ENDORSEMENTS
THE VALUE OF WORK

I have a personal habit of looking through the first 10 pages of a book, and if I do not find it interesting at that point, I won't waste my time reading it. When my friend, Douglas Woolley, gave me his book, *The Value of Work in the Eyes of God*, I began looking through it while I was on an airplane. The more I read, the more interested I became. As a businessman, I often ask myself "does my daily work really matter to God?" This book not only answers that question, but it biblically explains the "how" and the "why." When we work for God, He becomes our boss and our provider. Therefore, we will be motivated to do all our work with diligence and excellence, giving honor unto Him. It is workers like this that will point those around them to the reality of our Lord. Thank you, my friend Douglas, for this special gift of this book that opened my mind, and especially my heart, to these truths.

Mario Garcia Olvera
International President of Full Gospel Business Men's Fellowship International (FGBMFI)
Monterrey, Mexico

This book by Doug Woolley, *The Value of Work in the Eyes of God*, goes right to the heart of explaining why our everyday work is ordained by God in fulfilling His plan for our lives. Doug's literary ability is easily seen as he takes the reader from the history, theology, and biblical principles of work, to honoring God and balancing our individual significant priorities in life. He details the "Faith at Work Movement," and brings to light the misconception that we need to be ministering full-time to the spiritual needs of others, if we really want to please God. I pray the Lord will anoint your reading of Doug's book in discovering your work as a ministry.

Jimmy Rogers
Former President of Rogers-Wood & Associates, Inc.
Atlanta, Georgia

Doug Woolley succinctly traces the history of the Protestant work ethic through the contrasting attitudes currently held. This study of the theology of work has both breadth and depth with solid scriptural anchoring. Readers will be enriched with a deeper understanding of how time spent in meaningful work counts for eternity and glorifies God.

Dr. Royce Shelton
Professor Emeritus, Southeastern University
Lakeland, Florida

"The Value of Work is such an important book if we expect to reclaim our culture for Jesus Christ...The book you are holding in your hand will help fill the current void of solid materials on a theology of work" (from Foreword).

Os Hillman
President of Marketplace Leaders and Aslan Group Publishing
Cumming, Georgia

By carefully weaving the historical, theological, and practical aspects of work, Doug Woolley has been able to reveal to his readers the significant influence they can be in the marketplace. In my opinion, he has very clearly shown us that both the secular and the sacred are important to the carrying out of God's plans and purposes in the earth. This book is a must read not only for those in the workplace but should be read by those preparing to enter the workforce. I pray that this book will help its readers to understand more fully the verse, "And whatever you do, do it heartily, as to the Lord and not to men" (Colossians 3:23, NKJV).

Ed Russo
Senior Pastor, Life Church
Wesley Chapel, Florida

Many books have been written exploring faith and work issues, but helpful summaries of relevant biblical, historical, and theological perspectives are hard to find. In the book *The Value of Work in the Eyes of God*, Douglas Woolley provides us with a very useful introduction to the mountain of material he has been sifting through. He offers us a treasure-trove of information and a valuable introduction to some of the key people and perspectives that have shaped this movement.

Alistair Mackenzie
Teaching Fellow at Laidlaw College,
on Board of Directors of Theology of Work Project,
Founding Director of Faith at Work (New Zealand),
and author of Where's God on Monday?
Christchurch, New Zealand

Doug Woolley leaves no stone unturned in his research for *The Value of Work in the Eyes of God*. It took me back to God's promise to Abram, "…I will bless you… and you will be a blessing" (Gen. 12:2). *The Value of Work in the Eyes of God* details the "What" and the "How" of ministry in the workplace and, more importantly, it clearly lays out the "Why" we are called to be available to serve in all circumstances. Success in business is providing goods or services to help someone accomplish their goal, which is compatible with God's plan. Success in God's eyes is being available to be used by the Lord to serve in all circumstances. Doug Woolley's book is a valuable resource to accomplish God's goal for each of us.

Don Hayes
Former President of GTE Data Services and VP of GTE Information Technology
Former Director of Christian Embassy
Tampa, Florida

THE
VALUE OF WORK
IN THE EYES OF GOD

DOUGLAS E. WOOLLEY
Foreword by Os Hillman

XULON PRESS

Xulon Press
2301 Lucien Way #415
Maitland, FL 32751
407.339.4217
www.xulonpress.com

© 2021 by Douglas E. Woolley

Originally published in 2008 by Kingdom Concepts Publishing, Inc.

All rights reserved solely by the author. The author guarantees all contents are original and do not infringe upon the legal rights of any other person or work. No part of this book may be reproduced in any form without the permission of the author. The views expressed in this book are not necessarily those of the publisher.

Unless otherwise indicated, Scripture quotations taken from the New American Standard Bible (NASB). Copyright © 1960, 1962, 1963, 1968, 1971, 1972, 1973, 1975, 1977, 1995 by The Lockman Foundation. Used by permission. All rights reserved.

Paperback ISBN-13: 978-1-6628-0681-0

Ebook ISBN-13: 978-1-6628-0682-7

TABLE OF CONTENTS

Endorsements i
Foreword by Os Hillman xi
Introduction 1
    The Need 1
    Structure of the Book 4
    Personal Experience and Exhortation 6

Part 1: Review of the Literature 7

Chapter One:
Review of Books 11
    Purchased Books Dealing with Theology of Work 11
    Books Dealing with Practical
    Applications Derived from a Theology of Work 17

Chapter Two:
Review of Other Materials
and the Need for More Publications 23
    Professional Book Reviews, Journal Articles,
    Internet Articles, and Sermons 23
    Growth in the Number of Publications
    and the Need for More 25

Part 2: History of Attitudes about Work 29

Chapter Three:
Classical Period to the Reformation Period 33
    Classical Period: Greeks and Romans;

    Hebrew Jews and Christians 33
    Medieval Period: Secular versus Sacred 35
    Reformation Period: Reformers. 36

Chapter Four:
Enlightenment Period to the Current Period. 41
    Enlightenment Period and Industrial Revolution. 41
    Current Period 43

Part 3: Principles of a Biblical Theology of Work 47

Chapter Five:
Work is Full of Significance
When Connected with God. 51
    Definition of "Work" 51
    God is a Worker 51
    Humans are Created in the Image of God Who Works 52
    Creation Mandate – A Divine Command for Man to Work 53
    Sin Distorted Work in the Fall 55
    God's Redeeming and Transforming Work 57
    The Lasting Effects of Work 58
    Work in Eternity. 61

Chapter Six:
Purposes for Working 67
    To Glorify God. 67
    To Meet Personal and Family Needs 68
    To Help Others in Need 69
    To Benefit Society 69
    To Assist with the Great Commission 70
    For Personal Fulfillment. 71

Chapter Seven:
God Calls and Equips People to All Kinds of Work. 75
    All Legitimate Work has Significance to God 75
    Work as a Calling of God: A Vocation 76
    God Gives Abilities, Gifts, and Opportunities for Working. 82

Chapter Eight:
Work Ethics and Attitudes. 87

TABLE OF CONTENTS

    Laziness and Idleness are Sins 87
    Diligence 87
    Excellence 89
    Contentment and Joy 90
    Submissive, Faithful, Trustworthy, Respectful,
    and not Argumentative to Bosses 91
    Fair and Just toward Employees 92

Chapter Nine:
Balancing Work and Other Significant Priorities 93
    Balancing Work and Other Significant Priorities 93
    Rest and Leisure 95
    Retirement 97

Chapter Ten:
Christian Models for Understanding the Meaning of Work 101
    Vocational, Trinitarian, Charismatic, Ontological,
    and Collaborative Models 101
    Penitential, Creationist, and Eschatological Approach 102
    Theology of Creation, Anthropology, and Incarnation 102
    The "Integration Box" Model 103

Part 4: Faith at Work Movement 105

Chapter Eleven:
Background of Faith at Work Movement 109
    Defining the Faith at Work Movement 109
    Historical Progression of Faith at Work Movement 111

Chapter Twelve:
Profiles of Different Organizations 117
    The Founding and Leadership of Different Organizations ... 117
    Mission and Background of Different Organizations 118

Chapter Thirteen:
Some Practical Implications 139
    Implications from Teachings in Some
    Faith at Work Organizations 139
    Practical Thoughts about Career Decision and Work
    Connected to God 143

Conclusion 147
    History of Attitudes about Work 148
    Principles of a Biblical Theology of Work. 150
    Faith at Work Movement 153
    Closing Comments. 155
Tables 157
Glossary 159
Endnotes. 163
Works Cited. 195
About The Author 213

FOREWORD

Os Hillman

I began traveling and speaking about faith and work issues in 1996 after having a career in advertising. God led me to study the topic of faith and work and its role in the average person's life. I began writing and speaking on the subject. Since that time, I have been in twenty-five countries and spoken to hundreds of thousands of people about their calling in the workplace and the value it has by God. I have encouraged believers to know that their calling in their working life is a Holy calling, not a second-class calling. Now, twenty-five nations later and ten books later, I have learned one overwhelming fact: Christians do not have a theology of work. When I travel and speak, I often ask this question: "How many of you believe that your local church has effectively trained you to apply biblical faith in your working life?" The answer to that question consistently reveals only 10% of people respond affirmatively. The issue is not a question of being taught the Bible, for many of these respondents are in dynamic, Bible-teaching churches. It is a question of relevance. Churches have not been breaking down the Word of God for their average member in such a way that they can understand it and how it relates to their lives where they often spend 60-70% of their waking hours.

Without a theology of work, we cannot form a Biblical worldview. George Barna, in a 2003 survey found that only 9% of born-again Christians hold a Biblical worldview.

If that is true, how can we expect to see culture impacted for Jesus Christ?

Another survey done in 1998, conducted among a general population in the United States, asked the question: "Do you believe in God?" Of those surveyed, 93% of responders say, "Yes, I believe in God." However, when the findings were broken down among different industries the findings were very disconcerting.

Here were their findings:

- Military: 90%
- Business owners: 70%
- Politicians: 50%
- Arts and Entertainment: 3%
- Media: 2%

If you were like me, you were encouraged to see the top three categories reflective of a culture that believed in God. However, the last two categories are alarming. Arts and Entertainment and the Media are the two main industries that actually define culture. They shape what we believe and do not believe. Those operating in these industries do not hold any form of Biblical worldview and contributes to why we are seeing our culture move to being more liberal. All of this has a direct relationship to not teaching a theology of work in our churches, seminaries and Christian colleges.

The faith and work movement had its beginnings in the 1930s through CBMC (Christian Business Men's Committee) and the Full Gospel Business Men's Fellowship International (FGBMFI) that began in the 50s. This movement was an evangelical movement designed for Christian executives and professionals to have a platform for sharing Christ. The next phase of the movement began in the 80s and had a focus on applying the Word of God to *how* I do business. Founded in 1985, the International Christian Chamber of Commerce (ICCC) now operates in [75] nations; its focus was about applying the Bible to all aspects of work.

In the mid-nineties another shift took place. This was when groups like Pinnacle Forum and Bob Buford's Halftime came into being. These groups had a focus of impacting culture and the community through social entrepreneurship. Our organization, Marketplace Leaders, was birthed in 1996. The late nineties were also the time when the Billy Graham organization, Ed Silvoso, Dr. Henry Blackaby and Dr. Peter Wagner began to speak about this new move of God in the workplace. In the 2000s, we now see an emerging trend to help churches better equip men and women in their work life calling through groups like His Church at Work.

Today we are also seeing another trend to refocus our attention on helping Christians have a Biblical worldview. In 1975, Bill Bright and Loren Cunningham both got a "Word from God" as they put it. The word was that "if we expect to impact culture for Jesus Christ, we must focus our attention on seven mind molders (some say gates or mountains or pillars) of the culture. These include business, government, arts and entertainment, media, family, religion, and education. These seven sectors are the core sectors that define culture. "Win these and you win the culture," they would say.

In 2006 to our present time, we are seeing a birthing of teaching programs from groups like Focus on the Family that produced *The Truth Project*; Rick Warren, pastor and author of *The Purpose Driven Life* launched through his church, Saddleback, the Wide Angle: Framing Your Worldview program. Other notable ministries began speaking out and teaching about a biblical worldview and the need to focus on reclaiming the seven mountains of culture. Our organization, Marketplace Leaders, holds an annual conference on the theme *"Reclaiming the 7 Mountains of Culture."* These programs cannot have a solid foundation without a solid understanding of a theology of work. That is why Doug Woolley's book, *The Value of Work,* is such an important book if we expect to reclaim our culture for Jesus Christ.

The book you are holding in your hand will help fill the current void of solid materials on a theology of work. You will find this material thoroughly researched with a comprehensive review of the various theological views on work, its history from the early church to our present day, applications, and organizations operating within the area of faith and work. Individuals, universities, seminaries, and churches should use this book, as it provides solid understanding of God's view of our working life and why it matters to Him.

May you be enriched as you learn what the Bible says about our work and its importance in our world today!

Os Hillman
Marketplace Leaders

INTRODUCTION

The Need

Almost all adults work in some way—whether they serve as doctors, computer programmers, teachers, businesspeople, pastors, janitors, caretakers of dependents, or homemakers. Yet, 86% of American workers are "not satisfied with their job" and 82% are "unhappy with their work/life balance," according to a news release in 2004.[1] Similarly, surveys in Australia show that 80% of workers "find their jobs dissatisfying."[2] Many workers feel unfulfilled and frustrated in their work, including Christians. Work can be boring, mundane, stressful, and insignificant. Many do not see a bigger purpose for their work than simply earning money or meeting temporal needs of those served. While satisfying the needs of self and community are necessary, these purposes are ultimately unfulfilling if one does not sense a connection with God's purposes. Christians often feel that they waste the majority of their time on things that really do not matter in the grand scheme of God, and if they really loved God and people, they feel they should dedicate their lives wholeheartedly to God and minister to the spiritual needs of people on a full-time basis.

Most workers do not see a connection between what they do and what they believe God wants done in the world. A theology of work is necessary to see work from God's perspective and to realize that one's work is significant and valuable to God. Through the years, many have had a misconception that, in order for a person to be fully pleasing to God and serving Him, one has to go into full-time

Christian work by becoming a monk, a nun, a pastor, a missionary, a teacher of the Bible, a worship leader, or by performing some other ministry work. Since most people spend a majority of their waking hours at work, it is critical that Christians see their work as having significance to God and how it can be used to further His purposes on earth; otherwise frustration results. Christians desire meaningful work, which comes from work seen as service rendered to God, accomplishing His purposes as coworkers with Him, with results that outlast their mortal lives.[3] These meaningful connections appear in a proper theology of work.

Often, only those who work and contribute toward meeting the spiritual needs of people sense a clear connection with what God wants done on earth. Admittedly, an overall unifying message of the Bible is that God desires to redeem (and save) humankind and that He intervenes in history to do so,[4] often with the help of His followers. Therefore, people rightly see work that contributes toward the Great Commission of Jesus in **Matthew 28:19-20** as very important to God. However, many scholars today are making a biblical case that any person's work holds intrinsic value to God and can become a ministry to God and to others by working with the right attitudes and by sharing in word and deed. For God works and functions in other ways than just Redeemer, He also functions as Sustainer and Provider, for example. Thus, working to produce products and services that meet the needs of others is an extension of God providentially providing for His creation, and thus work is a ministry to people and unto God. Additionally, with God's empowerment, coupled with proper understanding and attitudes about work, Christians can turn their jobs into ministry by living out their faith at work in such a way that it attracts others to the God Whom they love and serve. Christians desire to see their work as a godly vocation, a divine calling, and a work that is valuable in God's eyes. Christians need a proper biblical view of work to guide them to proper actions and attitudes toward work, enabling them to use their work as a ministry and to see their work as a calling from God.

Although scholars have discussed the subject of work periodically throughout the centuries, formal "theology of work" books have only arrived on the scene since the mid-twentieth century. In the decades following, at least two dozen significant writings on theology of work appeared; yet, many have expressed the need to have scholars devote more time and effort in this new field to produce solid materials on a "theology of work," and for writers and pastors to subsequently make the results accessible to the common worker. Very few church congregations have ever heard a sermon that integrates faith principles with their professional work. Pastors and laypeople need to explore a theology of work and its practical implications, thereby coming to understand the value of work in the eyes of God and subsequently being motivated to proper work attitudes and habits.

To develop a good theology of work, scholars must address three particular areas: history, Scripture, and practical application.[5] First, scholars must consider the views and attitudes of the past toward work as they have contributed and shaped modern attitudes toward work. This especially includes learning from the wisdom of church theologians and scholars of the past, such as Martin Luther, John Calvin, and the Puritans. Second, scholars must consult the scriptural data to determine God's revealed view of work, as well as the comments of contemporary theologians concerning biblical passages. Third, scholars must integrate history and Scriptures with the real world to produce practical applications. Within this book, after reviewing the main literature pertinent to the topic, I present a theology of work and its practical implications by presenting historical views and attitudes toward work, scriptural data related to work, and practical ways to incorporate faith with work. Interspersed throughout the material and especially toward the end, readers may observe practical implications derived from insights gained from a scriptural perspective on work. Robert Tamasy sums up the essence of the biblical teaching on work and offers some eloquent insights:

> *Work is sacred. God ordained it from the beginning, before the fall of man. After the Fall, it just got tougher, frustrating, exhausting, sometimes even boring. Nevertheless, work pursued with excellence and integrity is still pleasing to God, a way of honoring Him by serving in the unique ways He has equipped us. Our work often provides the opportunities to proclaim Him to a broken, unredeemed world—through our example, as well as by our words.*[6]

Work is a gift from God to humanity, to share in His nature and His purposes for civilization.

Structure of the Book

The structure of this book consists of four main parts, which show the value of work in the eyes of God by exploring a theology of work and its practical implications. The first part gives an overview of the main books, journal articles, Internet articles, and sermons that exist on the subject and which I used as resources in the creation of this book. Scholars and others will certainly be interested in this overview that gives different authors' perspectives on work, while many others will want to skip this section initially to dive right into the "*History of Attitudes toward Work*" and then into the meat of the book that deals with "*Principles of a Biblical Theology of Work.*"

The second part of the book, "*History of Attitudes toward Work,*" traces the development of attitudes toward work throughout history, beginning with the Classical Period of the Greeks and Romans, progressing to the Medieval Period, to the Reformation Period, to the Enlightenment Period and Industrial Revolution, and finally to the Current Period. It is interesting to see the contrast of attitudes between the Greeks and Romans, who devalued work, and the Hebrew Jews and Christians, who valued work especially since their God was a worker who valued work. It is also fascinating to see how church leaders made a distinction between sacred work and secular work during the Medieval Period, and how the Reformers addressed this great division during the Reformation Period. After the Reformation Period had imbued work with spiritual significance, the Enlightenment Period and Industrial Revolution secularized the Protestant work ethic. Modern work attitudes stem from influences in the past, and while some today are workaholics, most prefer to get by with working as little as possible in order to maximize their leisure activities. In the Current Period, many Christians are confused about the value of their work in the eyes of God, especially in comparison to work done in church related activities. A proper theology of work helps bring clarity to this matter by showing that all legitimate work is valuable in God's eyes.

The third part of the book, "*Principles of a Biblical Theology of Work*," explores, and then answers in the affirmative, a vital question: Does human work have a divine purpose, meaning, significance, and value for those who labor, according to the Bible? After giving both a common and broad definition for work, this section presents the main aspects of a theology of work that contribute meaning to workers. First, God is a worker, and thus work is inherently good and meaningful. Second, God created humankind in the image of God who works. Third, man works according to a divine command, the Creation Mandate. Fourth, while sin distorted work in the Fall, work did not originate in the Fall as a curse for mankind. Fifth, God is interested in co-working with humankind in the transformation of society as well as personal redemption. Sixth, much of human work may resonate in the new earth. Work is full of significance when connected with God. Other important chapters deal with topics such as the purposes for working; an analysis of how all legitimate work has significance to God; work as a calling of God—a vocation; God giving abilities to work; work ethics and attitudes; balancing work and other significant priorities; rest and leisure; retirement; and different Christian models for understanding the meaning of work.

The fourth part of the book, "*Faith at Work Movement*," provides the background of the Faith at Work movement, profiles of different organizations within the movement, and some practical applications derived from messages emphasized in these organizations. Many organizations are serving people by helping them to integrate faith principles and their everyday work responsibilities. Some of these ministries focus on evangelism among workers while other ministries incorporate a more holistic approach to faith and work. These ministries are different avenues to assist people in implementing practical aspects of a "*theology of work*" into their lives.

In the Appendix and back area, the book contains a Table, Glossary, Notes, and a Works Cited section. The Glossary contains a definition of selected terms used in different parts of the book. The reader can reference the definitions upon encountering unfamiliar words used in the context of the Faith at Work movement or in the context of specialized theology. The Notes section is extensive and placed in the back of the book to allow easier readability of the main text. With rare exception, all the notes contain source citations instead of substantive notes with further verbiage on a particular idea. I have named the bibliography section, "Works Cited," since this book references all the bibliography items in the text or notes.

Personal Experience and Exhortation

As a committed Christian, working in the real world for a telecommunications company and two financial companies, I know firsthand how the principles of a theology of work have revolutionized my thinking about my job. Just as these principles have transformed my life over the years as I have explored the value of work in the eyes of God, so I also trust that these principles will transform your life as you incorporate biblical truths about work into your thinking, attitudes, and behaviors. Perhaps one of the many excellent "Faith at Work" type of organizations can channel you further in your desire to implement the practical implications of a theology of work. Perhaps you will lead others into a journey of exploration of seeing work from the vantage point of God. God is truly glorified as people work unto Christ, using their gifts and talents, with a purpose of serving others.

PART 1:
REVIEW OF THE LITERATURE

"…the purpose of work must be found in the value of its product…"

Dorothy Sayers

CHAPTER ONE
REVIEW OF BOOKS

Purchased Books Dealing with Theology of Work

In order to do the research necessary for writing about "Theology of Work," numerous books were purchased by me after searching online bookstores such as Barnes and Noble, Christian Book, and Amazon, using search criteria such as "Theology of Work," "Vocation," "Workplace Calling," and "Faith and Work," "Leisure and Sabbath," etc. I found other relevant books listed and described on workplace ministry sites, which provided book resources for integrating faith and work. I obtained many other books after reviewing descriptions of over seven hundred marketplace-faith books in *The Marketplace Annotated Bibliography*, written by Pete Hammond, R. Paul Stevens & Todd Svanoe.[7] More still, I purchased other books after seeing authors quote from particular books.

From these many purchased books related to the faith-workplace connection, a small percentage of them—perhaps two dozen—had as its focus a theology of work, though many had sections containing some elements of a theology of work. Most of the books emphasized **co-creationism**, where God exhorts man to participate with Him in His continuous work of creation. Although scholars have discussed the subject of work periodically throughout the centuries, the term "theology of work" first appeared around 1949,[8] and the first formal theology of work did not appear until 1950. In the decades following, at least two dozen significant writings on theology of work appeared.

Dorothy Sayers, an associate of C. S. Lewis, wrote the essay "Why Work?" in her 1949 book, *Creed or Chaos?* Which was first presented as a speech in England in 1942.[9] Sayers was one of the first to speak and write in modern times about a "right [biblical] attitude to work"[10] to an intellectual audience. According to Harrison, Sayers has a unique approach to work: "She focuses upon the end (*telos*) of work, arguing that the purpose of work must be found in the value of its product, which must be of such quality that it glorifies God. As creators, people must make themselves subservient to the work for which they are best suited in order to bring into being that which they were created to create."[11] "Central to Sayers's theology is the claim that we are called to be co-creators with God. Therefore, work must be understood as a participation in the reign of God and the value of our work defined by the quality of the product."[12] Sayers advocates that people must "estimate work not by the money it brings to the producer, but by the worth of the thing that is made."[13] The product of work is "the heart of Sayers's theology of work," according to Harrison.[14]

Josef Pieper's book, *Leisure: The Basis of Culture*, first published in 1948,[15] uses more philosophical arguments than theological arguments to emphasize that leisure instead of work is the basis for culture as it was for the Greeks, and it has "influenced subsequent theologies of work, especially those which have sought to resist and critique 'co-creationism.'"[16] Pieper sees leisure as being most meaningful when worshipful celebration is part of it.[17]

J. H. Oldham's book, *Work in Modern Society*, published in 1950,[18] "probably is the first formal theology of work...Oldham pleads for a lay-developed doctrine of work that will enable the majority of people to experience a genuine vocation to do ordinary kinds of work."[19] Alistair Mackenzie affirms the value of this "pioneering work" by saying "there is hardly a theme which has emerged in subsequent theologies of work which was not raised or prefigured in Oldham's writing."[20] Oldham first presents the realities of work-life in modern society so that people can properly assess and interpret a Christian meaning of work within that context.[21] With reference to **Genesis 1:28**, Oldham lays the groundwork for co-creationist thinking: "[Man] is commanded, that is to say, to co-operate with God in the continuance of His work in creation," and this decree remains even after the Fall.[22]

Alan Richardson's book, *The Biblical Doctrine of Work*, published in 1952,[23] focuses on the biblical material related to work with no attempt to apply the material to real life situations. Richardson's book laid the scriptural groundwork for many others to do a theology of work, "especially in more conservative Protestant circles."[24] Richardson says that the Bible does not encourage a connection between God's creative work and human creativity, though he does say that God did give man dominion over all creatures and creation, as described in **Genesis 1:28** and **Psalms 8:6**.[25] Instead, he sees work being a "divine ordinance for the life of man."[26]

Karl Barth's third volume, part 4, of *Church Dogmatics* published in 1961,[27] contains a section about "The Active Life" in which he presents a theology of work. He views work as a necessity of life for humankind that has some importance in that it is a command given to man,[28] but he rejects co-creationism. Barth cautions against over spiritualizing work and elevating it as worship.[29]

M. D. Chenu's 1963 book, *Theology of Work*, originally published in French in 1955, shows "man as collaborator in creation"[30] and gave movement to the "doctrine of cocreation that dominated the theology of work in both Catholic and Protestant traditions for the last half of the twentieth century."[31] With the revolutionary "changeover from craft tool to machine" that created different kinds of work, Chenu feels that traditional biblical images of "potter, blacksmith and peasant" are inadequate and often lead to "resentment against the machine," and thus a good theology of work must take these new technological innovations and concepts into consideration.[32]

Edwin Kaiser's book, *Theology of Work*, published in 1966,[33] is a full Catholic theology of work, drawing upon history and Catholic documents and advocating work as cooperation with God in his providence.

Gideon Goosen's book, *The Theology of Work*, published in 1974,[34] provides a positive view of work after tracing the historical views and attitudes toward work. Work is a God-given task for man to dominate the forces of nature and "collaborate with the Creator in continuing the work of creation," yet some work is "dehumanizing" and not creative and such activity should not be classified as work, according to Goosen.[35] True work produces a service to God and others.[36]

Jacques Ellul's book, *The Ethics of Freedom*, published in 1976,[37] has a section on "Freedom and Vocation," in which Ellul claims that the Bible does not speak of work as a vocation.[38] As an example, he says that **Genesis 1:28**, *"Replenish the earth, and subdue it,"* has no connotation of "divine vocation," but "we simply have to work—that is all."[39] Furthermore, for Ellul, work "is a result of the Fall" and "has no specific value" and "is a simple necessity" in life.[40] He also says, "Work is the painful lot of all men but it is not particularly important."[41] Consequentially, Ellul is opposed to a co-creationist view of work. "Clearly the ongoing battle between co-creationism and Barth and Ellul's view of work as necessity provides one of the main creative theological tensions in discussions about work and vocation during the last fifty years."[42]

Paul Marshall published his essay, "Vocation, Work, and Jobs," in 1980 in his book *Labour of Love: Essays on Work*.[43] After assessing historical views of work, Marshall describes vocation as a calling to be Christian in all spheres of life and not simply a call to a particular work. In addition, one should not be "obsessed with work" but should take a rest, for even God rested.[44]

Pope John Paul II encyclical letter *On Human Work*, published in 1981,[45] presents an updated view of work that, according to Leland Ryken, would be favorable to the original Protestants.[46] John Paul II presents work as having dignity[47] and as the expression of man, created in God's image.[48] He also promotes co-creationism.[49]

Dorothee Soelle, with Shirley Cloyes, wrote *To Work and to Love* in 1984,[50] where co-creationism is their framework for their theology of creation.[51] Soelle, with Cloyes, view the first creation as being unfinished and thus creation continues in an on-going process with the help of humankind.[52]

Doug Sherman and William Hendricks wrote *Your Work Matters to God* in 1987.[53] The heart of the book lies in presenting a theology of work, and it shows that secular work also matters to God. Its emphasis is that all work has intrinsic value to God and instrumental value to

God in that it is a means to accomplishing things that God wants, such as serving people's needs.[54]

M. Douglas Meeks wrote *God the Economist* in 1989,[55] arguing that "Economist" is a valid metaphor for the work of the triune God.[56] In his chapter on "God and Work,"[57] Meeks presents a Trinitarian perspective on work.[58]

Lee Hardy's book, *The Fabric of This World*, published in 1990,[59] attempts to "help revitalize the concept of work as vocation—or calling" (xv).[60] He does this by tracing the concept of vocation throughout history.

Miroslav Volf's book, *Work in the Spirit*, published in 1991,[61] is widely acclaimed for articulating a theology of work—one that is both eschatological and pneumatological.[62] After presenting a critical assessment of Luther's concept of vocation,[63] Volf proposes a theology of charisms, or gifts, which he feels is a "more stable foundation" to "erect a theology of work that is both faithful to the divine revelation and relevant to the modern world of work."[64] According to Volf, humans are coworkers with God, working in the Spirit with gifts from God, and subsequently, their current work has value not only in the present world but also in the world to come.[65]

Leland Ryken's book, *Redeeming the Time*, published in 1995, is an expanded and revised version of his 1987 book, *Work and Leisure in Christian Perspective*. The new book presents a theology of both work and leisure and how the two belong together. According to Hammond, Stevens and Svanoe, "This is perhaps the best and most integrated approach to daily life to date [2002]."[66]

Gary Badcock's book, *The Way of Life*, published in 1998,[67] provides a theology of Christian vocation, described as a way of life of loving God and neighbors.[68] Grounding human vocation in doing the will of God, Badcock says, "The will of God does not extend down to the details of career choice," thus liberating people to "live more adventurously...in an atmosphere of love."[69] God calls people to a life of love and discipleship.[70]

R. Paul Stevens's book, *The Other Six Days*, published in 1999,[71] presents a biblical perspective on vocation, work, and ministry. Stevens argues for a "people theology" that opposes the clergy-laity division and is for the notion that all are called to minister. Stevens balances both the Great Commission with the Creation Mandate and supports co-creationism.[72]

Alistair Mackenzie and Wayne Kirland wrote *Where's God on Monday?* published in 2003.[73] They present a theology of work that integrates faith with work in a popular way. Man is born to work as God's coworkers in line with co-creationism.[74]

Armand Larive's book, *After Sunday: A Theology of Work*, published in 2004,[75] presents a theology of work in line with co-creationism[76] and described by "work related characteristics of the Trinity"[77] that are initially distinguished in Volf's book and deepened and extended by Larive.[78]

Douglas Schuurman's book, *Vocation*, published in 2004,[79] attempts to renew a contemporary Christian doctrine of vocation and reshape it in light of important criticisms.[80] Schuurman addresses criticism over the theology of vocation by Badcock, Ellul, and Hauerwas, who say that scholars should not place religious meaning on secular life, and by Volf, who says that the traditional understanding of vocation is too static.[81]

Darrell Cosden's book, *A Theology of Work*, published in 2004,[82] presents dialogues with Jürgen Moltmann and Pope John Paul II to present a definition of work and a theology of work that consists of three dimensions: instrumental, relational, and ontological. Instrumentally, work is a means to provide for humans and to assist in a person's spiritual growth and sanctification; relationally, work provides self-fulfillment and impacts social relationships and civilization; ontologically, work itself has intrinsic, eternal value to God as an act of worship and a link to the new creation.[83]

Darrell Cosden's most recent book, *The Heavenly Good of Earthly Work*, published in 2006,[84] emphasizes how the Bible links present work to the new creation. Ordinary work and the things produced by it can be transformed and brought into heaven by God.[85] Thus, "all human work (and not just 'religious work') has eternal meaning and value."[86]

David Jenson's book, *Responsive Labor: A Theology of Work*, published in 2006,[87] "aims to recover a Christian theological vision of ordinary work, a vision that grounds human labor in God's initiating activity."[88] Human work is meaningful as it responds to God's work.[89]

Will Messenger is executive editor for the immeasurable *Theology of Work Bible Commentary* (Volumes 1, 2, 3, 4, 5), published in 2015 and 2016 by the Theology of Work Project, Inc. The combined one-volume hardcover commentary provide "an in-depth Bible study tool put together by a group of biblical scholars, pastors, and workplace Christians to help you discover what the whole Bible—from Genesis to Revelation—says about work."[90] Moreover, "It covers about 900 passages from all 66 book of the Bible, exploring what each passage says about work, workers and workplaces."[91] Thus, in addition to being grounded in a theology of the work, the commentary offers a springboard for genuinely practical application for everyday work.

Books Dealing with Practical Applications Derived from a Theology of Work

Upon further review of the books purchased, most of them fell in the category of popular writings that contained at least some elements of a theology of work, though usually emphasizing more practical applications or stories or testimonies. Dr. Peter Wagner had read and reviewed over 86 workplace ministry books by 2004, many of which were on my list, and he states, "One theme running through these books, especially the earlier ones, is how to be a good Christian out there in the workplace or in the 'world.' A later emphasis comes in defining a Christian's role in the workplace as 'ministry' *per se*."[92]

By 2006, Wagner had "purchased and read more than 100 books on the faith-at-work movement," thus his recent book, *The Church in the Workplace*, is a reflection of his views after surveying these other writings.[93] With this in mind and considering Wagner's influence in the lives of several influential spokespersons for the movement, such as Os Hillman and Kent Humphreys, his 2006 book is of great importance. His main point is that there are two forms of the one biblical church: "One is the gathering of believers in local church congregations each Sunday. The other is the scattered body of believers throughout the workplace the other six days of the week."[94] Wagner calls congregations the "nuclear church" and calls workplace believers the "extended church,"[95] having built "on the commonly accepted sociological concepts of the nuclear family and the extended family."[96] Each of these churches has a culture of its own and its own set of implied rules or assumptions, which can cause misunderstandings if not properly understood. Wagner feels that with proper understanding, appreciation, and support for the extended church, social transformation is possible.[97]

Os Hillman has been the most prolific writer in the Faith at Work movement. Coupled with his leadership role in the movement as president of two ministries, his writings are of practical importance. In 2000, Hillman published *Faith & Work: Do They Mix?*[98] where he contemplates from Scriptures and his own journey how to find purpose and meaning in one's work and to see work as a divine calling of God to ministry. In 2004, Hillman published *Faith@Work*,[99] which helps both pastors and church leaders understand the Faith at Work movement. In 2005, Hillman published *The 9 to 5 Window*,[100] which gives an updated overview of the Faith at Work movement and thoughts on how to connect a person's faith to their work life that typically occurs between 9 a.m. and 5 p.m.

Kent Humphreys' book, *Lasting Investments*,[101] guides pastors to help, in a practical way, their members who are workplace leaders to make an eternal difference in their sphere of influence, using their workplace as a platform for evangelistic and discipleship ministry. Similarly, Humphreys' latest book, *Shepherding Horses*,[102] helps pastors to understand the strong self-sufficient workplace leaders, whom he calls "horses," among the compliant sheep under the shepherd's care.[103]

Similar to Humphreys' analogy of workplace leaders as "horses," Linda Rios Brook uses an analogy of colored clothes in a laundry basket with the spiritual colors of church people and calls workplace leaders "the reds" in her book, *Front Line Christians in a Bottom-Line World*.[104] "The reds" want to lead[105] and will bleed on all other colors when they are wet by the "river of God," in an effort to "do church."[106] Brook makes the point that "the reds" are not fully understood or appreciated and often find the church irrelevant to their daily life, thus they desire to make an impact where they spend most of their time—the workplace—by establishing a non-traditional extended church at the workplace.[107] While most authors are not as pessimistic about current church environments, Brook demonstrates, as does Humphreys, that there is a need to recognize the unique qualities and desires of workplace leaders and for the nuclear church to equip them as "change agents" for work on the "frontline."[108]

David Miller's book, *God at Work*, published in 2007,[109] is a recent book to address the Faith at Work movement. It provides a scholarly study of the movement and its history. Additionally, Miller describes four ways to integrate faith and work using an "Integration Box" model consisting of *"Four E's"*: Ethics, Evangelism, Experience, and Enrichment.[110]

Building off the *Theology of Work Bible Commentary*, executive editor Will Messenger of the Theology of Work Project, has produced, from 2014 to 2015, *The Bible and Your Work Study Series*, which consists of multiple volumes on different topics, enabling a person or group to apply the Scriptures and Christian faith "to their work in positive practical ways."[111] Each volume in the series has multiple lessons, each "suited for Bible studies at work or with other people in similar occupations" during thirty-minute lunch breaks or other study times.[112]

"Christians can make an impact in the workplace with God"

CHAPTER TWO
REVIEW OF OTHER MATERIALS AND THE NEED FOR MORE PUBLICATIONS

Professional Book Reviews, Journal Articles, Internet Articles, and Sermons

I obtained twenty-three scholarly book reviews and articles related to "faith and work or career" or "vocation" from Southeastern University's Library via their online subscription service, EBSCO. In addition to various scholarly articles, the authors whose writings were reviewed in connection with a theology of work include the following: D. Michael Bennethum, John C. Haughey, Armand Larive, William C. Placher, Dorothy Sayers, and Miroslav Volf. Furthermore, while most of these authors had one review, three short reviews were for Larive and five reviews were for Volf, thus showing one indication of the importance of Volf's book, *Work in the Spirit*, in academe.

    I selected over seventy relevant articles from the Internet and read them thoroughly. I obtained many of these articles by performing searches in Google and Yahoo! using phrases such as "Theology of Work," "Vocation," "Faith at Work," "Spirituality of Work Movement," "Marketplace Calling," etc. Sometimes one link would lead to a set of insightful articles. I then found some relevant articles on ministry sites such as www.intheworkplace.com and www.faithatwork.org.nz. All the articles addressed aspects of a theology of work and viewed work itself in a positive Christian way, though two articles by Carly Friesen and Otto Helweg had an insightful alternative view in comparison to all the other articles. Carly Friesen in "Labor: Sin or Sacrament?" sees the Apostle Paul as emphasizing the suffering aspect of work, like Augustine and other church Fathers. Thus, according to Friesen, Paul embraces work not as "honorable" but as a "disgrace" revealing his personal weakness, so Friesen says, "The worker may have a sense of dignity in his toil because it is obedience to God in sharing the cross of Christ, but not because work *per se* is honorable."[113] Otto Helweg in "The Secular and Sacred; Friends or Foes?" sees "full-time Christian service" as the most spiritual calling and that God does not call people to secular tasks, for calling refers to spiritual gifts—not talents—to be used to build up the body of Christ.[114]

Having acquired thirty-seven audio sermons on work, I actively listened to them repeatedly in the car during a one-year period between 2006 and 2007. In 1993, while in Hong Kong, I visited the Asian Convention for Full Gospel Business Men's Fellowship International (FGBMFI). While there, I obtained the first sermon on audiocassette after seeing and hearing David Pawson deliver a message entitled, "Work."[115] Taking more notes during this sermon than any other sermon, I believe the message was life altering in giving a new perspective on work that I had not realized before that time. The message affirmed the value and dignity of work for its own sake and not just for its value in providing opportunities to witness. He encouraged Christians to "see that their daily work is full-time Christian service"—that does not need to be justified to God by witnessing at work, though Christians are called to be witnesses.[116] Pawson also emphasized the value of manual labor in particular, as the Bible often refers to God working with His hands as did Jesus, many of his disciples, and Paul.

Recently in 2005, I found an audiocassette message entitled "Why Work?" by C. J. Mahaney, recorded in 1991.[117] It also proved to be a life-changing sermon, giving the following as reasons for working: to love God, to worship God, to serve others, to develop character, to provide for one's needs, and to earn finances to invest.[118] These two sermons, coupled with reading and studying the book, *Your Work Matters to God*, in 2005, provided impetus for my undergraduate

Senior Project that would commence in 2006 and culminate into a book in 2008. I obtained all other sermons by searching the Internet for "Theology of Work sermons."

I acquired three excellent sermons from Gordon Kirk of Lake Avenue Church. The sermons dealt with a biblical view of employees, management, and work as an aspect of worship. Three more sermons came from Rich Lusk of Trinity Presbyterian Church. These sermons dealt with the connection of God and work, each emphasizing **Col. 3:22-24**. Ten other sermons came from Dr. Robert S. Rayburn of First Presbyterian Church, addressing such topics as vocation, duties of employees and employers, workaholics, leisure, and retirement. Nineteen sermons came from R. J. Rushdoony, with some focus on social transformation. Five messages came from a one-day workshop taught by Os Hillman, entitled *Called to the Workplace*. These messages showed how God meant for work to be a calling of God and a ministry.

I ordered two DVD's from available workplace resources for Christians, found on the Internet. Andy Stanley preaches six sermons in the series *Taking Care of Business* and hones in on the importance of working whole-heartedly unto the Lord. Os Hillman produced a DVD in 2005 entitled *God in the Workplace*, where he addresses the latest events in the Faith at Work movement and how Christians can make an impact in the workplace with God.

Growth in the Number of Publications and the Need for More

It is encouraging to see the growth in the number of publications for incorporating faith and work. Pete Hammond has stated that publication of books relating to the "faith-workplace connection" grew from 350 titles to 2000 titles, from the years 2000 to 2005, with the earliest books written in the 1930s. Many of these books focus on "leadership and management" and others speak to "issues faced by all Christian workers."[119] Over the past few decades, there has been an increase in the number of books focusing on theology of work, but there is still a need for more scholarly writings in this category.

Though there are at least two dozen good books dealing specifically with a theology of work, there is still a need for more academic writing in this field. Considering the importance of the topic and considering how its implications affect every working person, there should be much more research and writing done in this specific field. This is also evident, as different scholars in this field have also stated the need for more academic writings on the theology of work.

In 1955, M. D. Chenu wrote in his book *Theology of Work*, "Today, we are far from having achieved a 'theology of work,'"[120] yet he was pleased that "thoughtful Christians" were moving beyond just a study of "morality of work" that had been prevalent since the nineteenth century and to a necessary "study of work as a subject" itself.[121]

In 1974, Seward Hiltner expressed the need for a theology of work, "and quickly," to "take into account the impersonalization, dehumanization, and often degradation" that occurs more often than not.[122]

In 1993, Keith Harper said that there were very few who had produced a "definitive" theology of work, but felt that Miroslav Volf had now filled this void with his *Work in the Spirit*.[123] Two years earlier, in 1991, Miroslav Volf writes in his book that much more theological reflection takes place on ancient church debates, like transubstantiation, than on the matter of work that consumes the lives of most people.[124] Along similar lines, in 2004, Curtis Chang argues that writers have explored different theological positions for other subjects, but the lack of "schools of thought" on the subject of work indicates a sparseness of theological scholarship.[125]

In 2003, Jim Lewis, an Episcopal priest, says, "even though work plays such a dominant part in the Bible, one is hard-pressed to find much written today about the theology of work."[126]

In 2004, after writing his book on theology of work, Larvine says this topic is not yet well explored or a "mature area of theology."[127]

According to Dr. Peter Wagner, "Os Hillman is arguably the most broadly informed individual in the faith and work movement today. God is using Os to cast the vision for the church and the workplace for this new move of God in the body of Christ."[128] In 2005, Os Hillman acknowledged, "we have to have a good theology of work and this has been lacking, not only in the movement but in our churches."[129]

REVIEW OF OTHER MATERIALS AND THE NEED FOR MORE PUBLICATIONS

In 2006, Miller says, "With a few notable exceptions, most theologians do not develop interdisciplinary competence nor seek to understand the complexities of modern global economies and develop a constructive theology of work."[130]

In conclusion, it is encouraging seeing the growth of the number of "faith and work" books as well as seeing some recently published "theology of work" books. Yet, there is a clear need for more academic writing in this field, from which practical implications can be drawn and popular writings can be based to meet the real needs of the general public, most of whom work. Nevertheless, since the first publication in 2008 of my book, *The Value of Work in the Eyes of God*, the far-reaching "Theology of Work Project" completed its five-year mission that was just starting: The *Theology of Work Bible Commentary* was a culmination of more than five-years of research by 140 contributors from sixteen countries, guided by a steering committee of twenty international scholars, pastors, and Christians from a variety of workplaces, co-chaired by Dr. Haddon Robinson, fifth President of Gordon-Conwell Theological Seminary and a foremost preacher in the English-speaking world, and by Mr. Thomas Phillips, an effective corporate leader and biblical/theological teacher.[131] The Theology of Work Project's research material (consisting of Bible commentaries, Bible Study series, Devotionals, Podcasts, and Online resources)[132] were published and made public in 2015, and now people are able—more than ever—to produce books, teachings, and sermons to equip common workers with the truths and implications of a theology of work. Along similar lines, it is my hope that my current book will also help assist others to have a transformed view of work, in accordance with Scripture, and provide a basis for others to produce further books, teachings, and sermons to better equip others in the area of work.

PART 2
HISTORY OF ATTITUDES ABOUT WORK

"Scriptures commanded diligent work for all able-bodied people and condemned idleness"

CHAPTER THREE
CLASSICAL PERIOD TO THE REFORMATION PERIOD

Classical Period: Greeks and Romans; Hebrew Jews and Christians

During the Classical Period, the Greeks despised work and viewed it as a curse—an evil to be avoided. The Greeks considered work to be "beneath the dignity of a free person."[133] According to Plato and Aristotle, the highest form of life was the "contemplative life of the mind,"[134] so the "elite devoted themselves to the exercise of the mind in art, philosophy, and politics."[135] Work distracted people from freely exercising the mind, thus philosophers saw work as demeaning.[136] To be in a state where one did not have to work for the necessities of life was highly valued as it allowed one to pursue more worthwhile activities, such as being a politician or a military hero, that helped them become immortalized like the gods.[137] While manual work was devalued, study and contemplation were valued as helping man to ascend to the gods.[138] The Greeks regarded work with one's head as superior to work using one's hands. They had an ambition to work as little as possible to maximize their leisure pursuits.[139] In quest of a life of happiness, Greeks had a lofty view of leisure whose goal was "contemplation and the life of the mind" while the Romans also valued leisure but "preferred active pursuits, including physical fitness and spectator sports."[140]

Like the Greeks, Romans despised labor, according to Kaiser, largely due to their desire to be independent from having to work for others—either out of necessity or out of gain.[141] Roman agriculture or farming became associated with slaves, who soon outnumbered freemen, and thus people despised farming along with all kinds of work performed by slaves.[142] Since slaves did most of the labor, Friesen says, "Labor came to be equated with slavery in the minds of the people."[143] Thus, both Greeks and Romans had a negative view of work, seeing it reserved primarily for slaves.

"Unlike the Greeks, who thought that working for one's living was beneath the dignity of a gentleman, the Hebrews looked upon daily work as a normal part of the divine ordering of the world, and no man was exempt from it."[144] Because Yahweh worked, work in Hebrew culture had value far above work in Greco-Roman culture.[145] The Old Testament and Hebrew culture did not elevate intellectual work over manual work, and even Rabbis who studied also worked at a trade for financial support,[146] like Jesus (**Mark 6:3**) and Paul (**Acts 18:3**). Balancing intellectual pursuits with physical skills, almost every Jewish boy was taught how to work with his hands in a trade to support himself financially.[147]

In New Testament Christianity, work is esteemed further as its primary characters served as manual laborers: Jesus as a carpenter; some disciples as fishermen and a tax collector; and Paul as a tentmaker (**Acts 18:3**).[148] Jesus identified with the common worker through his parables. Also, Scriptures commanded diligent work for all able-bodied people and condemned idleness even while hoping for the soon dramatic return of Jesus (**Col. 3:23; 2 Thess. 3:10**). Christianity "gave slaves and workers value as people who God loved."[149] This positive view of work was the prevailing Christian attitude for the first century after the Apostles.

Medieval Period: Secular versus Sacred

"Gradually the Church Fathers began to draw more heavily on Greek and Roman motifs in their theology and the more positive view of work gave way to a much lower view."[150] Ordinary secular work became less valued as it was distinguished from religious work. Eusebius in the fourth century is known to have divided life into two spheres, one indicative of the sacred and the other more secular. Emphasizing suffering in work as part of the curse,[151] Augustine distinguished between the "contemplative life" (*vita contemplativa*) of reflection and religious meditation and the "active life" (*vita activa*) of common work with a preference for the former as being of a higher order.[152] This crucial distinction and attitude ran throughout the Middle Ages.[153]

During the Medieval Period, a two-tiered concept of work developed where life was divided into two spheres: "the sacred spiritual life of contemplation and the secular world of labor," where contemplative "spiritual" work was considered far superior to physical earthly work. The work of priests, monks and nuns was "spiritual" and of a higher order than ordinary work, and people could only enter their work by a divine calling.[154] "The highest human endeavor was to meditate and lead a solitary life" and thus the common worker built and supported monasteries.[155] In the eleventh century, church rules imposed celibacy upon the clergy and thus "the demarcation between priesthood and laity was complete" and rendered ordinary workers as second-class citizens to the clergy who had a higher spiritual status.[156] According to Guinness, elevating spiritual work over secular work is a distortion of the truth of calling, which he calls the "Catholic distortion" since it "rose in the Catholic era."[157]

In the thirteenth century, "Thomas Aquinas, in his *Summa Theologica*, defended the spiritual hierarchy of the Middle Ages with significant implications for the world of work."[158] Aquinas developed this pyramid hierarchy theory of society using Greek thoughts—writings from Aristotle who built from Plato's writings.[159] Though all work was necessary, Aquinas's hierarchy of work placed "spiritual works" such as prayer, preaching, and the like in a higher rank than "manual works" which were also ranked according to profession and trade.[160] Calhoun says, "This view is reaffirmed and elaborately developed by Antoninus of Florence (A.D. 1486-87)."[161] While acknowledging that all Christians have a calling in a general sense, only the work of the church was deemed a vocation.[162] Vocation in the Medieval Period "meant being called into the 'spiritual order' with its special privilege of greater closeness to God by its abundance of good works."[163]

Reformation Period: Reformers

In addition to the dignity given to work with one's hands during the Renaissance,[164] the Reformers dramatically developed a very positive view of work. Martin Luther rejected monasticism and the well-established division between "sacred work" and "secular work."[165] People used the word "vocation" exclusively for a call to monastic life, thus implying that "God did not call other people to their jobs"[166] and their work had "little if any spiritual significance."[167] "The Reformation made [vocation] a universal term, applicable to all states of life and all kinds of work. All work is regarded as a service to God. In principle, all kinds of work are 'holy,' in so far as they are performed in faith and in obedience to God."[168] Thus all work, sacred and secular, intellectual and manual, were ways of serving God.[169] Therefore, Luther said that it was not necessary to leave or escape secular work and go into church work to be "pious" or pleasing to God, as was previously thought.[170]

According to Goosen, while Luther encouraged staying in the same vocation with no personal ambition, John Calvin provided for the opportunity to change vocations in order to better utilize one's gifts and talents and to serve neighbors and saw no evil in personal ambition or "moving into better jobs or up the social ladder."[171] In favor of capitalism, "Calvin encouraged workers to produce more than they needed so they could give surpluses to those in need."[172] Calvin had a more positive view of the world and its potential than Luther, so for Calvin, Christ is the "transformer of culture."[173] "Calvin... taught that believers are responsible for social transformation, and his followers began to believe that we have a cultural mandate (the mandate to transform society) as well as an evangelistic one (the mandate to save souls)."[174]

The Puritans carried the Reformers' message, and historians know the Puritans for their Protestant work ethic. The Puritans were exemplary, according to Packer, in integrating faith into their daily lives—a holistic lifestyle—where all awareness, activity, work and enjoyment had the purpose of honoring and glorifying God.[175] They emphasized diligence in their work, as stewards of God's call, whose purpose was to serve God and society.[176] "The Puritans commended industriousness and profit in moderation."[177] The Puritan's Protestant ethic of hard work produced thriving societies and "later fueled the industrial revolution which produced vast increases in invention, productivity, and wealth."[178]

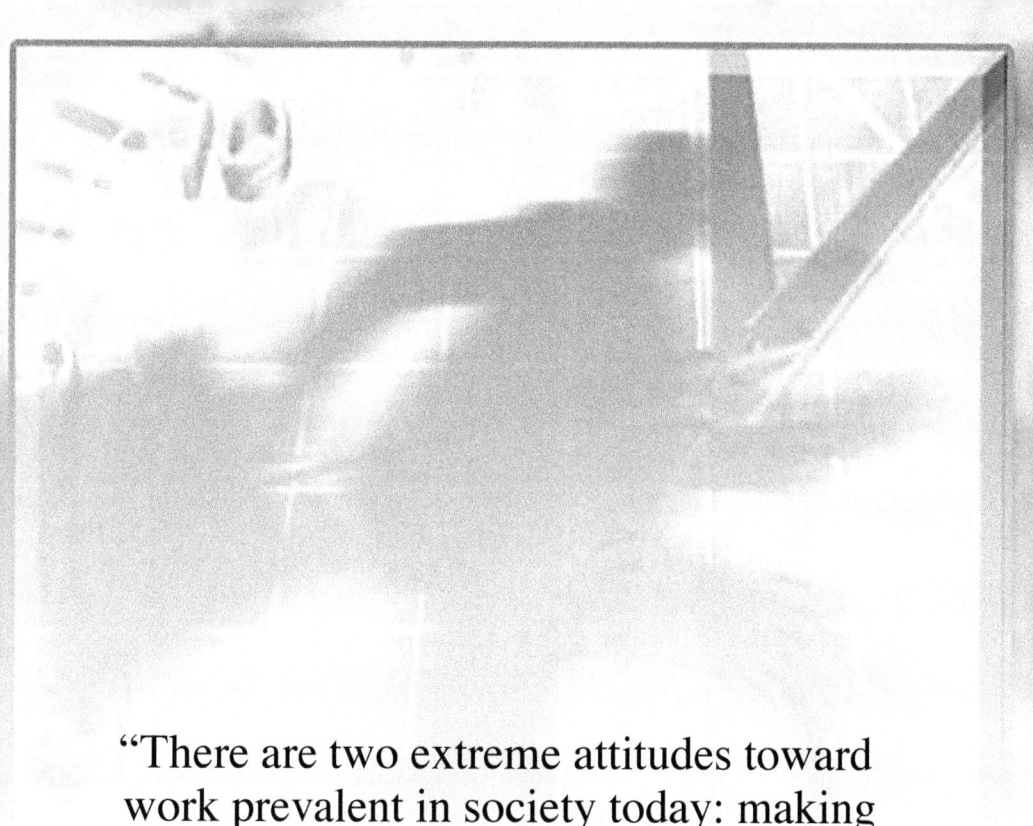

"There are two extreme attitudes toward work prevalent in society today: making too little of work and making too much of work"

CHAPTER FOUR
ENLIGHTENMENT PERIOD TO THE CURRENT PERIOD

Enlightenment Period and Industrial Revolution

While diligent hard work remained in the work ethic, the Puritan's original focus on working unto Christ disappeared and thus a vocation really became just an occupation with no connection to God. Imbelli observes the potential for this oscillation saying, "bringing the religious and secular into close conjunction" by having vocation or calling assimilated to work and occupation "can serve either to enhance the secular or domesticate the religious."[179] During the Reformation, secular occupations were enhanced, but the Enlightenment secularized spiritual callings. This removal of the spiritual from secular work and subsequent elevation of secular work is called the "Protestant distortion" by Guinness.[180] The eighteenth-century Enlightenment brought a humanistic "ethic of self-interest and expediency," thus "perverting" the original Protestant ethic "into a creed of personal success."[181] In the secularized version of the Protestant work ethic, Lee Smith says, "there was no central purpose to glorify God, no concept of stewardship or servant hood, and no moral duty to help the needy."[182]

The Industrial Revolution of the nineteenth and early twentieth centuries used machines to increase production, which formed "alienated workers" on an assembly line that continuously focused on a specific task that became monotonous, and they were not able to see how their never-ending work fit into the end product.[183] Karl Marx describes such a person as "a cog in the wheel" of economic activity.[184] Marx encouraged workers to look for personal fulfillment in the work of one's hands, which eventually led to idolizing work. Marx's friend and associate Friedrich Engels "increasingly glorified work as an end in itself," thus "the worker and his work have taken on religious significance" within Marxist countries.[185] Marxism believed that the working class, by reforming institutions, would redeem society, yet such a system has not succeeded in Communist countries that have tried it.[186]

Since the time of modern industrialization, more and more women have sought work outside the home. Some have done so to acquire needed income, yet others search for a meaningful occupation. Addressing a Women's Society in 1938, Sayers says, "It is very well to say that woman's place is in the home—but modern civilization has taken all of these pleasant and profitable activities out of the home, where women looked after them, and handed them over to big industry, to be directed and organized by men at the head of large factories."[187] Some of those traditional activities that required "head as well as hands" included "spinning, weaving, baking, brewing, distilling, perfumery, preserving, pickling...[and being] in command of her own domestic staff."[188] Thus, "the home contains much less of interesting activity than it used to contain."[189] In Sayers opinion, "It is perfectly idiotic to take away women's traditional occupations and then complain because she looks for new ones"[190] even outside the home. Yet, many mothers stay at home with their kids realizing that it is an important function and responsibility to train and raise them and it can be intellectually stimulating as well.

Although society transferred much meaningful work from the home to the factory as industry grew, Simmons says, "There are modifications [people] make to [their] activities and purchasing habits to restore some of that meaningful activity."[191] For example, instead of purchasing bread and products, one bakes bread and grows food.

In addition, "there seems to be a revival in recent years of home-based activity and industry" with the ability to telecommute, thanks to the technology of modems and the Internet.[192] Thus, women can potentially do interesting work at home, and parents who prefer to stay at home with their children have that option.

The value given to secular work has oscillated since the Reformation. Around 1800, the modern missionary movement started with an emphasis on evangelism and the "evangelistic mandate, but not so much the cultural mandate."[193] By the end of the 1800s, liberals promoted the "social gospel" and went to the "extreme of advocating that [work of] transforming society was all that was necessary and that saving souls was an idea of the past."[194] Bible believing evangelicals reacted to this extreme by going to the other "extreme of rejecting social ministry [work] altogether."[195] In the 1950s and 1960s, Wagner was probably like many other evangelicals when he says, "I was of the persuasion that our task was to save souls, make disciples and multiply churches. Period."[196] In 1974, in Lausanne, Switzerland, the evangelical movement held the International Congress on World Evangelization. "Evangelicals began reconsidering the place of the cultural mandate alongside the evangelistic mandate within the total mission of the church...[though] subordinating the cultural mandate to the evangelistic mandate."[197] This viewpoint was an important shift from an exclusively evangelistic emphasis that many evangelicals had. Thus, Evangelicals considered secular work as important too.

Current Period

There are two extreme attitudes toward work prevalent in society today: making too little of work and making too much of work, which Pawson calls "immorality" and "idolatry," respectively.[198] Many view work as a necessary evil, something to be avoided, in order to maximize their leisure time. They want to make as much money as possible while working as little as possible. According to Pawson, this "attitude leads to other forms of immorality of the workplace" such as "the evasion of tax, calling in sick when you are not sick, [and] taking company property home as if it's your own."[199] On the opposite extreme, others idolize work and derive their identity and security from their work. They will work long hours and sacrifice other important things such as their family, relationships, and church activities. People can find the biblical view of work between these two extremes.

Mark Greene believes that the greatest cultural challenge facing the church today is "SSD Syndrome," that is the "sacred-secular divide," "the pervasive belief that some parts of our life are not really important to God—work, school, leisure—but anything to do with prayer, church services, church-based activities is."[200] With that thinking, holy people go into sacred work while less holy people do secular work and become second-class spiritual workers. Others believe there is no difference in God's eyes between sacred and secular work, and thus there is no hierarchy of occupations, like full-time Christian work being more spiritual or pleasing to God than secular work. A.W. Tozer believes that all work can be just as sacred as that of a minister because, "it is not what a man does that determines whether his work is sacred or secular, it is why he does it." The motive is everything. Let a man sanctify the Lord God in his heart and he can thereafter do no common act."[201]

Despite verbally acknowledging that their purpose in life is to glorify God, most Christians struggle with the meaning of their ordinary work "in comparison with what they do on Sundays or in activities typically associated with the spiritual, the ministry-oriented, or the 'eternally' important."[202] John Beckett in his book, *Loving Monday*, expresses his work attitude that is common to many Christians:

> *For years, I thought my involvement in business was a second-class endeavor—necessary to put bread on the table, but somehow less noble than the more sacred pursuits like being a minister or a missionary. The clear impression was that to truly serve God, one must leave business and go into "full-time Christian service." Over the years, I have met countless other business people who feel the same way.*[203]

Attitudes toward work in today's society vary from hating work to loving work. Those who hate their work often see work as an evil necessity whose main purpose is to acquire money to afford leisure. Many people are aware they are underemployed—where their college degree does not serve them in the job market today.[204] Ryken says that those who are underemployed are quite numerous and represents some of the most dissatisfied workers since they are too highly educated, or too physically able, for their jobs.[205]

According to Mahaney, people can observe current attitudes toward work in culture by reading some humorous bumper stickers. For example, the phrase "I owe, I owe, so it's off to work I go" indicates that people only work because they need to pay their bills; they work for materialism and the purchasing of possessions. If they win or inherit a large sum of money, then they would not work. Their purpose is not serving people through their work but making money to afford things and leisure opportunities. Several bumper stickers show people's dissatisfaction with work and their desire for leisure including "Take this job and shove it," and "Thank God it's Friday." In addition, people can see a depreciation of work and the exaltation of leisure in the phrase "A bad day at golf is better than a good day at work," and the commercial where a man on a camping trip, with others, raises a beer triumphantly in his leisure activity and says, "It just doesn't get any better than this." Society says that a fulfilled life is to be found in the context of leisure, not work. Culture and society bombard people with messages from commercials, billboards, movies, and TV shows, saying that work is "not honored," but a "drudge."[206] Many see work as undesirable and unfulfilling, and people long for early retirement. A lottery winner may say, "I never have to work again," as if that is the goal.[207] Yet, Christians should not reflect these attitudes. There should be a distinct difference in the attitudes and motives and goals of Christians toward work. Work is not just about the paycheck, but it is about serving people and God, who instituted work.

PART 3:
PRINCIPLES OF A BIBLICAL THEOLOGY OF WORK

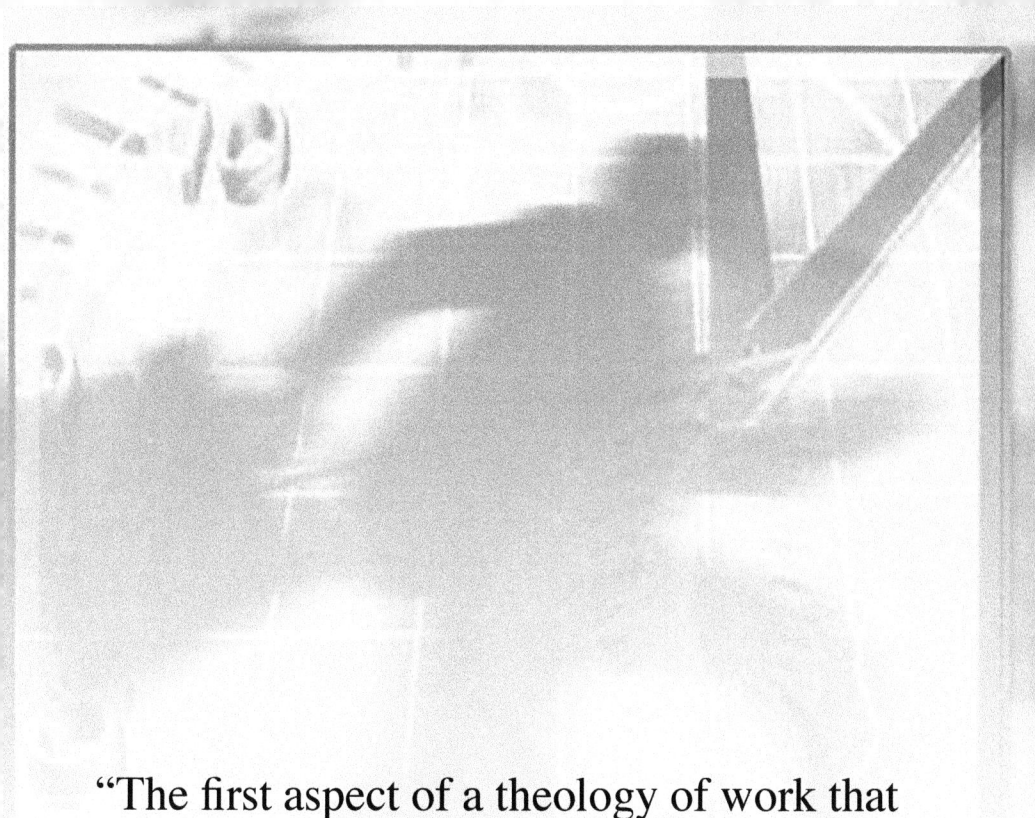

"The first aspect of a theology of work that provides meaning for human workers is that God Himself is a worker"

CHAPTER FIVE
WORK IS FULL OF SIGNIFICANCE WHEN CONNECTED WITH GOD

Definition of "Work"

In defining *work*, society and authors often refer to *work* as "paid employment." While the Bible addresses this aspect of work, the Bible also uses words for work that encompass broader definitions that embrace dominion over nature, service to others, and all productive activity. Geldard defines work in this broader way as "the investment of one's energy in dominion over nature and the service of others."[208] Stevens also defines work in a broader way as "purposeful activity involving mental, emotional or physical energy, or all three, whether remunerated or not."[209] As a result, businesspersons, manual laborers, homemakers, volunteers offering services, and God are all individuals who work. The Bible discusses aspects of a theology of work.

God is a Worker

The first aspect of a theology of work that provides meaning for human workers is that God Himself is a worker, and thus work has intrinsic value. God was the first worker who created, designed, fashioned, engineered, molded, and constructed the entire universe.

The Bible says, *"In the beginning God created the heavens and the earth"* (**Gen. 1:1**). The first two chapters of Genesis show God actively at work, creating all that exists, and His work is characterized as *"good"* (**Gen. 1:10, 12, 18, 21, 25**) and *"very good"* (**Gen. 1:31**). Yet God continues to work even after the initial week of creation. Paul acknowledges God in Christ as creator of all and that *"in Him all things hold together"* (**Col. 1:17**). The psalmist declares that God *"who keeps Israel will neither slumber nor sleep"* (**Ps. 121:4**). Jesus said, *"My Father is working until now, and I Myself am working"* (**John 5:17**). Thus, to sum up the biblical references, Paul Minear aptly says, "The God of the Bible is pre-eminently a worker."[210]

God's activities associated with creating the heavens and the earth and all their hosts describe His "work" (*mela'khah*) in **Genesis 2:2**. This same Hebrew word is used to describe man's work in the Ten Commandments (**Ex. 20:9-10**), thus showing a connection. Throughout the Bible, God describes His initial and ongoing work using images from the world of human work. Robert J. Banks explores sixteen of these in his eight-chapter book, *God the Worker*, including God as composer and performer, metalworker and potter, garment maker and dresser, gardener and orchardist, farmer and winemaker, shepherd and pastoralist, tentmaker and camper, builder and architect.[211] These images are very helpful in connecting one's work on earth with the kind of work God does. Therefore, unlike some societies in history that devalued work because their pseudo-gods favored contemplation instead of activity, work on earth has dignity because the almighty God works. Work is valuable in the eyes of God, and God created humans to work in partnership with Him.

Humans are Created in the Image of God Who Works

The second aspect of a theology of work that provides meaning for human workers is that God created humans in the image of God Who works, and thus humans have a nature to work. God, who works, created man in His image: *"Then God said, 'Let Us make man in Our image, according to Our likeness'...And God created man in His own image, in the image of God He created him; male and female He created them*" (**Gen. 1:26-27**). God did not create any other creature in God's image. Pope John Paul II rightly says, "*Work is one of the characteristics that distinguish* man from the rest of creatures, whose activity for sustaining their lives cannot be called work. Only man is capable of work."[212] The capacity to work is certainly a key characteristic of man and should be a prominent feature of the image of God along with the more customary features.

With reference to other passages found later in the Bible, the image of God can refer to "*righteousness and holiness*" (**Eph. 4:24**) and to beings that are "free, rational, capable of self-appreciation and self-expression, [and] capable of moral and spiritual understanding."[213] "While [Sayers] accepts that a case may be made for the divine image being found in the 'immortal soul,' 'rationality,' or 'self-consciousness' (all of these quite traditional locations of the *Imago Dei*), she argues that the author of Genesis had none of these in mind."[214] As Sayers mentions in *The Mind of the Maker*, the main thing known about God in the first twenty-six verses of Genesis chapter 1 is that God creates. Since verse 27 says man and woman are created in the image of God, then a main characteristic shared by God and humanity is that of being creative, which Sayers calls "the desire and the ability to make things."[215] Clearly, humans do not create things out of nothing, *ex nihilo*, like God does.[216] Explaining Sayers' view, Harrison says, "God retains the capacity to bring into existence from non-existence, while humans can only order that which already possess being."[217] Humans have a desire to work creatively, which Patrick Reardon articulates expressively by saying that humans are "hot-wired to want to be productive."[218] Thus, since creative work is part of God's nature and character, creative work is also a part of humans' nature and character.

Creation Mandate – A Divine Command for Man to Work

The third aspect of a theology of work that provides meaning for human workers is that God gave a divine command for man to work, in partnership with Him to accomplish His purposes, also called the Creation Mandate. Throughout the Scriptures, the Bible shows work to be a divine ordinance for human life.[219] In **Genesis 1:28**, God commanded Adam and Eve to "*fill the earth, and subdue it; and rule over*" all living things. The words "*subdue*" and "*rule*" imply active work and, according to Julian Doorey, "responsible dominion."[220] Alistair Mackenzie and Wayne Kirkland say this verse places a stewardship role upon humans whom God calls to work with Himself to further His purposes. "Because of this, the value and significance of our work is directly related to how connected it is with God's work."[221] Part of God's work is providentially caring for the earth and its people; in a practical sense, God uses people and entrusts them with this purposeful work.

The Bible gives the Creation Mandate to manage the earth's resources and meet human needs in **Genesis 1:28**. The Bible further expresses this in **Genesis 2:15** as "God took the man and put him in the Garden of Eden to cultivate it and keep it." The Hebrew word for "cultivate" or "till" is *avadh*, meaning to work or to serve, and the word "keep" means "taking pains 'to care for.'"[222] Thus, man came into partnership with God: God planted the garden (**Gen. 2:8**), and man cultivated it (**Gen. 2:15**).[223] In addition to working in and caring for the garden, God gave man the enjoyable intellectual activity of naming the animals (**Gen. 2:19**). God made woman to help man in his God-given tasks (**Gen. 2:18**). Commenting on **Genesis 2:15-19**, Stanley M. Horton says, "Adam was given work to do, such as cultivating, trimming and caring for the garden (otherwise the garden could have become a jungle). This work would be healthy and also a joy, thus, God made him a responsible being sharing in part of the work of taking care of God's creation."[224] The mandate given to man was to share in God's work and be His coworkers and partners, cooperating with God. Such work carried significance and meaning.

Although work prior to the Fall was surely different, and certainly enjoyable, a few writers take the position that such work was not considered labor. To an extreme, French layman Ellul holds that Adam did not really work prior to the Fall, at least not in the current sense of the word: "Rather he plays. All is given to him by God."[225] Although most English versions translate **Genesis 2:15** to say that God put man in the garden "to work it and take care of it," John Sailhamer prefers Umberto Cassuto's translation "to worship and to obey."[226] In Gordon Hugenberger's scholarly article on **Genesis 2:15**, he lists four arguments they use for such a translation; then he provides six detailed arguments against their translation and in favor of the traditional translation by analyzing Hebrew grammar and biblical references.[227] Although the nature of work was different prior to the Fall, the Bible shows that man was given responsibility for purposeful, active work as a coworker with God.

In addition to the creation narratives affirming the call of God for man to work,[228] the Bible shows work to be a divine ordinance in many other parts of the Scripture. The fourth commandment recognizes that man's nature is to work; he is to work six days (**Ex. 20:9**) and rest on the seventh. According to Richardson, this commandment surely means, "an honest week's work is every man's duty."[229] Additionally, **Psalms 104:23** recognizes that man works at his labor until evening. The book of Proverbs is full of exhortations for diligent work and warnings against idleness: *"Go to the ant, O sluggard, Observe her ways and be wise"* (**Prov. 6:6**). Several New Testament Scriptures show work as a moral duty and reveal the attitude Christians should have in their work: **Colossians 3:22-4:1; Ephesians 6:5-9; 1 Timothy 6:1; Titus 2:9; and 1 Peter 2:18-25**. Thus, work is a divine ordinance and command, carrying with it purpose and meaning from the greatest employer.

Sin Distorted Work in the Fall

The fourth aspect of a theology of work that provides meaning for human workers is the realization that work did not originate from the Fall, but was instituted by God prior to it; thus, work is not a curse. However, because of man's sin, work was distorted in the Fall. God declared in **Genesis 3:17-19**: *"Cursed is the ground because of you; in toil you shall eat of it all the days of your life. Both thorns and thistles it shall grow for you; and you shall eat the plants of the field; by the sweat of your face you shall eat bread, till you return to the ground."* Commenting on **Genesis 3:17-19**, Horton says, "God put a curse on the ground (not on Adam). What had been pleasant work would now become toil, often unrewarding, often difficult because of thorns and thistles."[230] The curse came upon the soil, the work field that man is to cultivate, but Goosen says it also affects all kinds of work—mental and physical as seen in **Matthew 13:3-23, 24-30; Galatians 4:11;** and **Isaiah 43:24**.[231] Drudgery and monotony now characterize all manual, mental, and spiritual work.[232] When **Genesis 3:19** says, *"By the sweat of your face you shall eat bread,"* Harrison says, "suddenly, human survival comes to depend upon work and productivity."[233] Furthermore, God evicts man from the Garden of Eden, according to **Genesis 3:23**, *"to cultivate the ground from which he was taken."* Clearly, man had to work hard after the Fall.

Some would contend that work is a result of the Fall and part of the curse. To substantiate this argument, some have argued that man did not really work prior to the Fall, but played as Ellul says,[234] or he worshipped and obeyed as Sailhamer and Cassuto believe.[235] Therefore, according to Ellul, work is a consequence of the Fall[236] and thus has no intrinsic value and cannot be regarded as a vocation or a calling of God. Yet almost all English versions and theologians properly translate the early **Genesis** verses to say that man was working prior to the Fall. According to Raymond O. Bystrom, "It is important to emphasize the dignity of work today because many believe Christianity teaches that it is the penalty for sin or God's retaliation for our rebellion...Most biblical exegetes acknowledge that work is not the legacy of the Fall, only its character as toil."[237] Man worked prior to the Fall, and in spite of man's rebellion causing the task of work to become more difficult, God continues to require man to work after the Fall—the divine ordinance will continue to stand to the end of history.[238] Work is certainly less meaningful when viewed as a curse upon humankind instead of originating as an ordinance from God. With a proper understanding that work originated from God prior to the Fall and that God desires people to still work according to His purposes, work becomes meaningful and significant. In addition, according to Wayne Kirkland, the Fall does not change the Creation Mandate; instead, it adds a further responsibility to humans' role as coworkers, and now mankind assists God in His redeeming work, which includes the restoration of creation to God's original intention.[239]

God's Redeeming and Transforming Work

The fifth aspect of a theology of work that provides meaning for human workers is that God is redeeming and transforming all of creation and man gets to partner with Him in this divine purpose. God is in the process of redeeming not just souls but also all of creation. As Mackenzie and Kirkland say, "He intends to transform and redeem everything and everyone—all that he brought into being"[240] as mentioned in Paul's letters to the **Romans (8:18-23)**, **Ephesians (1:9-12)**, and the **Colossians (1:15-20)**. An overall theme in Colossians, according to Lusk, is the preeminence of Christ and that God is reconciling all things to Himself through Jesus (**Col. 1:20**), and the latter part of the letter shows some of the areas to be reconciled: husbands and wives (**3:18-19**), children and parents (**3:20-21**), employees and employers (**3:22-25, 4:1**).[241] God has committed Himself to saving the whole creation, and He is interested in working toward that end even now.[242] Thus, man cooperates in God's work when he helps to redeem and transform creation, which includes evangelism—leading people to a personal faith in Jesus as Savior and Lord. "Everything we do to counter or reverse the effects of the Fall is a participation in God's redeeming and transforming work and looks forward to the completion of that work."[243]

As centuries have passed, types of work have changed and made work a bit easier. Although a Utopia will not be established by means of technological or socio-political advances, Richardson says "It is not wrong to attempt by means of technological or other improvements to reduce the sheer drudgery of labour; surely the contrary is true, that it is our Christian duty to remove in any way we can 'the curse of Adam', to eradicate the 'thorns and thistles' and to wipe off the 'sweat' from the face of man."[244] Though God will not remove the curse fully until after Jesus returns (**Rev. 22:3**), Christ's death on the cross affects every area of life: because of His redemption, "work as a blessing prevails over work as a curse."[245] Gordon Kirk says, "Work can be redeemed, even in the fallen world. Anything that helps us overcome the effects of the pain, the hardship, the difficulty, is part of this redemption. Work itself retains some of the quality of the curse, but the attitude of the worker [in Christ] can transform the work."[246] C. J. Mahaney agrees that transforming one's attitude will transform one's job that may be boring and repetitive, and he says that transformation of one's attitude comes by understanding the transcendent God who created people and His gift of work and His command to work and its purposes.[247] Any work on earth that emulates God's work, such as redemption and transformation, carries significance, purpose, and meaning for the worker. Three factors contribute to whether or not a person views human work as helping to form the "final" Kingdom: one's view of the goodness of the current world, eschatology, and the new earth to come.

The Lasting Effects of Work

The sixth aspect of a theology of work potentially gives work an eternal purpose if the effects of work remain throughout eternity on the new earth, which depends on three factors, one of which is how one views the current world. If one views the world as good, then the potential exists for man to achieve dominion by working hard and ruling and subduing the earth as God originally commanded. **Psalms 24:1** says, *"The earth is the Lord's and all it contains, the world, and those who dwell in it."* Additionally, a good world opens the possibility of helping to establish the final Kingdom on this earth through human work. Alternatively, others view the earth as Adam's fallen world and thus people will never be able to fully rule and subdue the earth and achieve dominion, as God commanded Adam.[248] Not even the great and wise King Solomon could fully exercise dominion in a lasting way, as he also lived under the curse in a fallen creation under judgment. Solomon describes work as frustrating and futile, but work is also a gift that people can enjoy.[249] In its present condition, the world does not seem conducive for man to build gradually the final Kingdom without revolutionary changes accompanying the dramatic return of Christ.

Eschatology plays a role in whether work has eternal value. The purpose of "Christian mission" is "to transform reality around it," according to missions expert David Bosch.[250] Depending upon one's view of eschatology, the object emphasized for "transforming" varies: premillennialists emphasize saving the individual soul—focusing on the personal—transforming the individual; and postmillennialists emphasize saving society—focusing on the social—transforming society.[251] Theologians have developed three main eschatological views: amillennialism, supported mostly by historic Protestants and Catholics; postmillennialism, supported by some Evangelicals and Charismatics, mainline and liberal Protestants, and ecumenical groups such as National Council of Churches and World Council of Churches; and premillennialism, supported by most Baptists, Holiness groups, and Pentecostals along with conservative Evangelicals.[252] Most premillennialists "saw little hope for society before Christ returned to set up his kingdom";[253] therefore, the Social Gospel and social transformation seemed futile and unwarranted. Their emphasis has been on personal salvation and often includes transformation of personal behaviors. "Post-millennialists believe that the Saints, empowered by the Holy Spirit, will bring in the great harvest and build the Kingdom, preparing the way for Jesus' glorious return."[254]

According to Miller, premillennialists have increasingly "moved toward a hybrid position, gradually accepting the importance of saving society, as well as souls."[255] Evangelicals have had to struggle between the two biblical mandates of evangelization in the Great Commission (**Matt. 28:19-20**) and social concern in the Great Commandment (**Matt. 22:37-39**). While evangelization has had priority over the years, consensus has been reached at the 1974 Lausanne conference and ultimately at the 1983 World Evangelical Fellowship for Evangelicals to include both evangelism and social transformation in its church mission statement.[256] Thus, humans participate in God's work as they serve both souls and society. Most within the differing millennial views "believe that God will establish a new Earth surrounded by Heaven where the Saints will work, rule and live with Christ forever [**Isa. 65:17-25**]."[257]

Both a view of the goodness of the earth and eschatology culminate in the third essential criteria for determining if work has eternal value: one's view of the new earth. Scripture is clear that there will be "*a new heaven and a new earth*" (**Rev. 21:1; 2 Pet. 3:13; Isa. 65:17, 66:22**), but there are two theories as to how this will come about. John F. Walvoord holds that "the present earth and heaven are destroyed and will be replaced by the new heaven and new earth"[258] by an "act of new creation" and not by renovation.[259] J. D. Pentecost also holds this view.[260] The alternative theory, held by Herman A. Hoyt, is that God will form a new heaven and earth by a "change or rearrangement" of materials in the present heaven and earth.[261] W. A. Criswell also holds this view and says "this earth is our home forever and forever into the ages of ages,"[262] since the new heaven and new earth will be the same heaven and earth as now but will be "redeemed," "regenerated," "renovated,"[263] "remade, washed, cleansed and purified."[264] Analogous to the previous findings, Andrew McDearmid says, "The scholars I have consulted are about equally divided between the two theories."[265]

Whether or not the current earth will remain throughout eternity is crucial in the thinking of recent theological developments concerning work by Volf, Goosen, and Cosden, who argue that work has eternal value as a means of establishing the new creation. "If the world will be annihilated and a new one created *ex nihilo*, then mundane work has only earthly significance," according to Volf, and "human work is devoid of direct ultimate significance."[266] Instead, Volf argues for the eschatological transformation of the world, where many human works will be "cleansed from impurity, perfected, and transfigured to become a part of God's new creation."[267] In opposition to the annihilationist view, Goosen reiterates, "Positive and redeemed work will continue into eternity (not just any work)."[268]

In addition to God redeeming the immaterial soul, God will also redeem material bodies and the physical creation, as a corollary to the Incarnation that established the goodness and importance of material creation.[269] According to Goosen, "Just as the material world shared in man's Fall, so too it is called to participate in the new heaven and new earth."[270] Creation groans in anticipation (**Rom 8:22**) of being reconciled and transformed (**Col. 1:20**) into the new creation. According to Volf and his graduate school mentor Jürgen Moltmann, the new creation should always be the concern of the Christian faith that is insistently eschatological.[271]

Cosden in *The Heavenly Good of Earthly Work* strongly believes that all work and the things produced by work "can be transformed and carried over by God into heaven."[272] Furthermore, "Ordinary work affects and in some ways actually adds to (though it does not cause, determine or bring about) the ultimate shape of eternity—the new creation."[273] According to Cosden, Christians should value what God values, which are those things that He will save eternally.[274] Arguing from Jesus' Resurrection of His material body, Cosden says that, "in addition to people, human work and the material creation are to be part of God's salvation."[275] Some may feel that work is exerted and then gone forever, but just as "God can raise and transform the dead," he can also "raise and transform all present and even past (decayed and gone) earthly realities" from work, which He then purifies and integrates into the fabric of the new creation.[276] If work does last beyond a person's mortal life and does contribute to the world to come, as Volf, Goosen, and Cosden contend, then such labor has further significance, purpose, meaning, and value.

Work in Eternity

Although there is a facet of work that ends when this life ends (**Rev. 14:13, John 9:4**), there will also be work in eternity, described as serving (**Rev. 22:3**) and reigning (**Rev. 22:5**). The tasks for which God assigns in eternity will not have the toilsome effects of the Fall as the curse will be removed (**Rev. 22:3**). Kirk believes work in eternity will be like it was prior to the Fall and illustrates this future work as being like a fun hobby that one enjoys doing.[277] According to Goosen, "There are no images in the Bible to suggest a heaven of glorious immobility," an idea influenced by Greeks whose idea of a perfect state is "immobile, unchangeable, and static."[278] The most frequent image for heaven is that of a wedding feast, which is not a passive event but a joyous celebration.[279] Heaven will have a perfect balance of contemplation and activity. Although biblical descriptions of eternity are scarce, there are enough pictures "to excite anticipation for this glorious future."[280]

With the few descriptions and pictures given in the Bible about the future life coupled with an overall theological understanding of the Bible, Christians have generally held two views concerning the future life. The first view focuses "on the fulfillment of the believer's relationship with God and see[s] worship and praise as the primary if not exclusive activities of heaven."[281] The second view, "while not excluding worship, tend[s] to emphasize reunion with family and friends, social relationships, and activities of service and work."[282] John Jefferson Davis does a good job arguing a case in his essay that "there will be *new work* for the redeemed people of God to do in the New Creation, and that worship will be a central but not the exclusive activity in the world to come."[283]

Since the New Creation is a creation of God, God will continue to work by sustaining the New Creation.[284] Further, "God's essential nature as a free, creative, and omnipotent being will never change throughout eternity; God the Creator will still be creative in the New Creation."[285] Davis reasons further saying, "Since man, as the image of God, was created to mirror the nature and works of God, it follows that if God continues to work in acts of creation and providence, redeemed humans in the New Creation will continue to reflect the Creator by caring for fellow creatures and by engaging in new, creative acts of art, invention, culture, and worship."[286] Work was given to man prior to the Fall, so work is not inherently burdensome or a punishment, but it is "a privilege and opportunity to reflect the character, activity, and creativity of the Creator."[287] Since work is inherently good and was given to man in the original creation, and since "the New Creation is the fulfillment of God's original intention," God will restore His original intention of work for humans in the New Creation, and thus new work will be a feature of the new world to come.[288] Although the New Creation will not need God's work of redemption, His work as Provider and Sustainer will continue since humans, animals, and plants will remain as creatures, which, "by definition, have needs that must be met by others."[289] Only God is totally independent and self-sustaining; "all creatures depend on God and, secondarily, on other creatures for their existence, life, and health."[290] Humans can once again participate in God's work of providence by creatively meeting the needs of others and caring for the New Creation.

Because of the Fall in the Garden of Eden, a curse was placed upon the earth by God (**Gen. 3:17-18**), but in eternity there will "*no longer be any curse*" (**Rev. 22:3**). To remove the remnants of the curse, God will purge the existing heavens and earth (**2 Pet. 3:10, 12; Rev. 21:1**) and create a *"new heavens and a new earth, in which righteousness dwells"* (**2 Pet. 3:13**), which is the "final preparatory act anticipating the eternal kingdom of God."[291] "This passing of the present earth is anticipated in a number of passages (**Matt. 24:35; Heb. 1:10-12; Rev. 20:11**)."[292] Dave Hunt believes that endless life will reside not on earth but in heaven[293] which he describes as "a new universe of absolute perfection"[294] or of "bliss."[295] However, since Jesus Christ will be dwelling among His people in eternity (**Rev. 21:2-3; John 14:3; 1 Thess. 4:16-17**), J. D. Pentecost concludes that "the eternal abode of the church" will be "in the new earth, in that heavenly city, New Jerusalem."[296]

Pentecost says, "Our occupation in the eternal state will not be with our position or glory but with God, Himself."[297] Just as work was part of paradise in Genesis—not idleness, Mahaney emphasizes, "Eternal life is not going to be eternal idleness...It will not be boring, it will not be repetitious, and it will not involve idleness. There will be a work involved because it is part of the character and nature of God as a creator and because God works and because we are made in His image, we will want to work too!"[298] According to Criswell, "Every indication points to our increasing responsibilities in a New Jerusalem" and gives an example of the parable of the pounds where the Lord blessed faithful men and placed them in authority over cities.[299] Moreover, "In that celestial civilization each man shall have his place according to his faithfulness in this world and in this life."[300] Commenting on Jesus' servants who serve Him in **Revelation 22:3,** Walvoord says, "This is a picture of blessedness in service rather than of arduous toil."[301] Hoyt says, "The attitude of worship will permeate every aspect of activity and employment."[302] Hoyt mentions three areas of responsibility and development engaged in by the redeemed: "the area of administration requiring the exercise of wisdom" (**Rev. 22:5**), "the area of exploration requiring the gift of investigative curiosity (**Rev. 21:24, 26**)," and "the area of creative and productive."[303] Regardless of the kind of activities assigned, the tasks will surely bring great fulfillment and happiness to the worker.

"For activity to be glorifying to God, it must be in obedience to either a command or request of God"

CHAPTER SIX
PURPOSES FOR WORKING

To Glorify God

Many theologians would say that the purpose of life is to glorify God, in essence to please Him, for all things were created according to God's will and for His pleasure and glory (**Rev. 4:11**). The Apostle Paul says, "*Whether, then, you eat or drink or whatever you do, do all to the glory of God*" (**1 Cor. 10:31**). For activity to be glorifying to God, it must be in obedience to either a command or request of God or, at least, not be immoral to God. Work has biblical precedence as a divine command and ordinance for humankind (**Gen. 1:26, 2:15, 3:23; Eph. 4:28, 6:5-7; Col. 3:23-24**; etc.). Thus, work is an activity of life that people should do for the purpose of glorifying and pleasing God. Rick Warren believes that people should do everything, including work, to the glory of God: "By doing everything *as if you were doing it for Jesus* and by carrying on a continual conversation with him while you do it...Work becomes worship when you dedicate it to God and perform it with an awareness of his presence."[304] For the Bible says to workers, "*do all in the name of the Lord Jesus*" (**Col. 3:17**) and "*Whatever you do, do your work heartily, as for the Lord rather than for men*" (**Col. 3:23**). Furthermore Peter encourages people to work to glorify God, "*As each one has received a special gift, employ it in serving one another...so that in all things God may be glorified through Jesus Christ*" (**1 Pet. 4:10-11**). Although some activities and work would be morally unacceptable to God, such as stealing or prostitution, almost all work in society is legitimate in God's eyes as it meets the needs of families and society or maintains His creation.

To Meet Personal and Family Needs

The Bible says that people are to work to meet personal needs. Paul says, in **1 Thessalonians 4:11-12**, to work so as to *"not be in any need,"* and thus be able to purchase the necessities of life and to pay any bills consistently on time. Lee Smith warns, "Of course it is necessary to distinguish between actual needs and selfish desires. It is easy for us to fall to the temptation of materialism, greed and the selfish satisfaction of our appetites."[305] Laboring hard enables one to have money to pay for daily *"bread"* (**Prov. 12:11**) or meals (**Prov. 16:26**) and *"not be a burden"* to others (**2 Thess. 3:7-8**). To avoid poverty, one must labor (**Prov. 14:23**).

Another purpose for working is to meet the needs of one's family. A person responsible for a household has an obligation to provide for them, thus the Scriptures exhorting one to work to meet personal needs extends to meeting the family's needs. In **1 Timothy 5:8**, Paul says, *"If anyone does not provide for his own, and especially for those of his household, he has denied the faith, and is worse than an unbeliever."* In **Mark 7:11**, Jesus says it is wrong for a man to set aside money to God, as a "Corban," that is needed by his aged parents since God desires him to obey the commandment to honor father and mother (**7:10**). Also, **1 Timothy 3:3-4** says that it is important to be *"free from the love of money"* and to manage one's household well. Those who have responsibility for a family are required to work for money to meet the needs of the family and not lavish it on themselves; they must be good managers of the limited money or resources for the wellbeing of the whole family.

To Help Others in Need

Working provides resources for one to help others in need. Paul encourages a person to labor *"in order that he may have something to share with him who has need"* (**Eph. 4:28**). While the Bible is not against a person prospering as a result of being successful at work, it does warn that wealth and riches should not be one's goal or motive in working (**1 Tim. 5:6-10; Prov. 23:4**). Instead, one should be content with God's blessings, enjoy them, and share generously with those in need.

To Benefit Society

Society is dependent upon workers exchanging goods and services. In God's providence of sustaining creation (**Isa. 42:5-6; Heb. 1:3; Col. 1:17; 2 Pet. 3:7; Matt. 6:33; Rom. 8:28**), He meets the needs of society—Christians and non-Christians—as each person works in his/her particular field for the common good. Paul exhorts people to *"do good to all men, and especially to those who are of the household of the faith"* (**Gal. 6:9-10**). Paul strongly reprimands able-bodied Christian members of society who act like "busybodies" and refuse to work: *"if anyone will not work, neither let him eat"* (**2 Thess. 3:10-12**). According to Hillman, "There is value in secular work simply because it meets needs found in society. God created mankind with many different gifts and talents to serve the multifaceted needs of human beings."[306] "Work in the Christian view is inseparable from service to our fellow-men," for man lives in community and not in isolation and thus has responsibility for his neighbor.[307] To love one's neighbor, as God requires, one must serve his neighbor through work. "Work has a Christian meaning only if the occupation is one by which society is truly served...From the point of view of service to one's fellows[,] manual and spiritual work are on the same level."[308] Through work, God wants to meet the various needs of people, both physical and spiritual, both temporal and eternal. Even if the product of the work is temporal, those who benefit from it are eternal.[309] Peter Stuart makes the point that workers also meet human needs indirectly by caring for God's creation, and not raping the earth, as it is important for human survival.[310] Christians should view their daily work of serving others in society as an expression of loving their neighbors, for love meets practical needs.[311]

To Assist with the Great Commission

Prior to His ascension, Jesus gave the Great Commission, *"Go therefore and make disciples of all nations, baptizing them in the name of the Father and the Son and the Holy Spirit, teaching them to observe all that I commanded you"* (**Matt. 28:19-20**). Work facilitates this evangelistic task in two ways: as a means to make and give finances toward evangelism and as a means of engaging in personal evangelism. First, work provides a means of making money to finance those in vocational ministry who spend their time preaching the gospel with little or no remuneration (**Phil. 1:3-5; Phil. 4:15-16**). Lee Smith says, "Compensating those who give their lives to evangelism and the spiritual nurture of Christians is clearly valid and expected in the New Testament" (**1 Tim. 5:17-18; 1 Cor. 9:3-14; Gal. 6:6; 3 John 5-8**).[312] A partnership forms in the holy work of spreading the gospel when other workers support gospel workers. Freeing others for gospel work is a great reason to work, according to James Davidson.[313]

Second, work can be a means to evangelizing—both in action and in word. According to Mark Greene, "The workplace is the one place where Christians can't avoid contact with non-Christians," and the workplace is the area where non-Christians can really see the difference that Christ makes in a Christian's life over a period of twenty to fifty hours a week for several years.[314] According to **1 Thessalonians 4:12**, work is a good testimony toward nonbelievers who expect believers to also support themselves and their own families by the work of their own hands. By honoring a boss and working hard for him or her, one can be a good witness for God (**1 Tim. 6:1**). Moreover, Paul says, *"Urge bond slaves to be subject to their own masters in everything, to be well-pleasing, not argumentative, not pilfering, but showing all good faith that they may adorn the doctrine of God our Savior in every* *respect"* (**Titus 2:9-10**). Performing work and performing it well and with respect for the boss and coworkers, can be a good witness for Jesus. Yet, no matter how wonderful the action, people cannot really interpret such actions as a witness for Jesus without some measure of verbal witness to explain the reason for the action.

Christians can view work as a platform for verbal evangelism; thus, Christians consider coworkers, customers, and clients as a mission field. It is hard to be a good verbal witness for Christ if one is not already a good worker that has earned the respect of others. To have spiritual influence in the workplace, Peel and Larimore say Christians must demonstrate competence, character, and consideration prior to courageously engaging in wise communication.[315] Christians should *"always be ready"* to give an answer to those who ask about their faith (**1 Pet. 3:15**).

Some authors caution against seeing the workplace "only" as a context of winning people to Christ, as if the work itself does not matter to God: life and work are broader than just evangelism, and work has intrinsic value.[316] Why should working people receive the gospel? Many would say, "To be saved and go to heaven." Yet, according to Rayburn, God also desires the gospel to restore humankind to the spiritual condition that enables them to fulfill their original purpose as given in the Creation Mandate. Thus, the Great Commission does not replace the Creation Mandate; instead, it enables humankind to fulfill the Creation Mandate.[317] People who become Christians should desire to share the gospel with others, but their new Christian nature should also enable them to do their work according to God's original intent.

For Personal Fulfillment

Work is a gift from God and should bring personal fulfillment. Carol Haywood takes this further saying, "Work is necessary for fulfillment" and "may be a basic right of a human being," instead of a curse, since the institution of work preceded the Fall.[318] Nevertheless, reality is that not everyone enjoys their work, nor is everyone using all the talents God gave them to perform the type of work they are doing. Due to the Fall, work is often frustrating and boring. Nevertheless,

King Solomon says that work is a gift from God (**Eccles. 2:24, 3:13, 5:18-19**) and can be seen as good by putting work in its proper perspective. Lee Smith provides such a perspective: "Using our God-given abilities and opportunities to be useful and to accomplish tasks is rightly satisfying. Work meets needs for self-esteem and a sense of personal worth. There is a sense of satisfaction found in constructive work to meet our needs, help others and support the work of the ministry locally and globally."[319] Thus, joy and satisfaction should come from working. Furthermore, Solomon says, *"And I have seen that nothing is better than that man should be happy in his activities, for that is his lot"* (**Eccles. 3:22**).

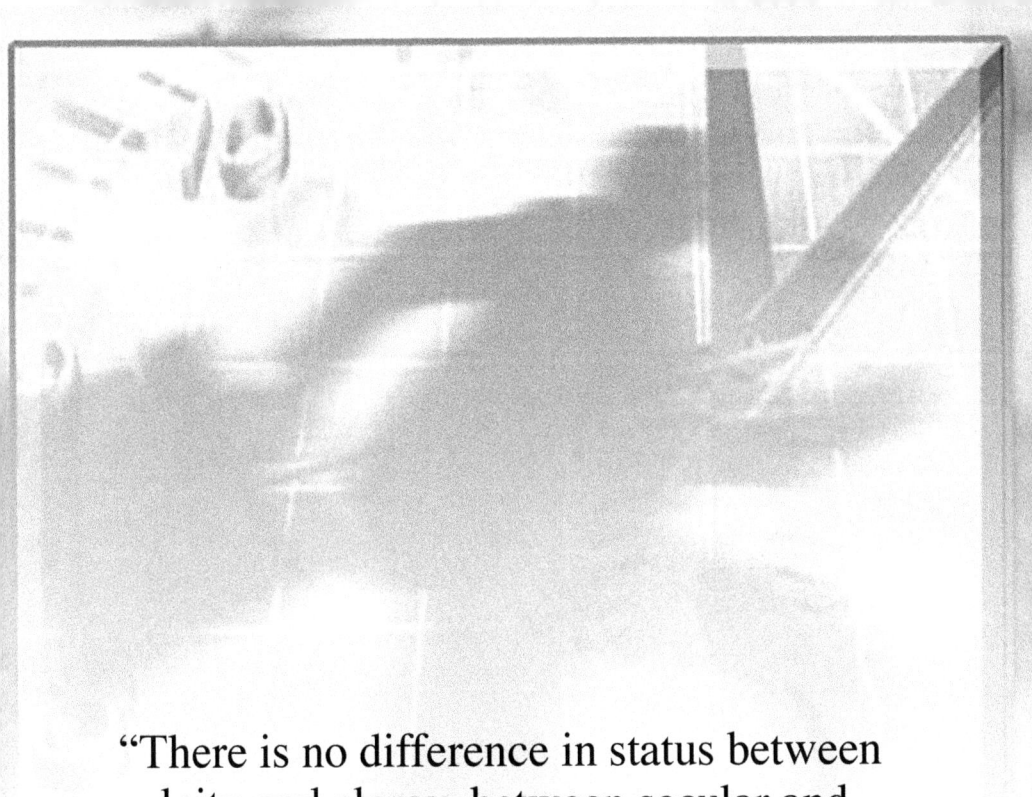

"There is no difference in status between laity and clergy, between secular and sacred jobs, for all workers are called to minister unto God"

CHAPTER SEVEN
GOD CALLS AND EQUIPS PEOPLE TO ALL KINDS OF WORK

All Legitimate Work has Significance to God

For many people, there exists an unconscious hierarchy of occupations, with some being more spiritual than others, or more pleasing to God than others. Church ministry is clearly an important work for which God designed some people. With reflection on the Protestant ethic that declared the "sanctity of all legitimate work in the world, no matter how common," Ryken says, "no vocation, including church work, is regarded as more 'spiritual" or more pleasing to God than other types of work."[320] The Anglican Church Diocese of Sydney issued a resolution 50/95 stating that everyday work is just as valuable to God as vocational ministry:

> *This Synod recognizes, encourages and supports the roles of Godly men and women in their everyday work vocation– as distinct from ordained or full-time ministry–and affirms its belief that such work of service in and to the world, done in the name of the Lord Jesus and by God's enabling, is true and laudable service rendered to God Himself by*

those whose vocation and ministry it is, and is no less acceptable to Him than the Ministry of the Word.[321]

Moreover, Arthur Wallis says that Larry Peabody's book, *Serving Christ in the Workplace*, "proves that there is no scriptural authority for the belief that serving God in business is any less spiritual than serving God in full-time ministry."[322] According to Hillman, all occupations are equal: "The key is to be in the place where God has called you and to live for the glory of God in that place."[323]

Work as a Calling of God: A Vocation

During the Medieval Period, people saw a vocation exclusively as a divine call to religious work, or the monastic life. Against this background and in protest of it, Martin Luther formalized and popularized the concept of vocation in which there is no division in the eyes of God between sacred and secular positions, or occupations, and that God calls people to all kinds of tasks in the world.[324] Luther considered all work and all of life as a vocation, a calling from God to express faith and love in serving others. Anyone could have an occupation, but according to Luther, only Christians could have a vocation—spiritual work—that involved worshiping God and lovingly serving one's neighbors for their sake.[325] Work was only good if it served neighbors, which thus served God.[326] Thus, for Luther, monastic work was evil since it did not lovingly serve others, only self,[327] but an executioner was not evil since it was a means of maintaining order in society.[328] Making good products for their own sake was not adequate; people had to make the products because their neighbors had a need. Thus, Luther's doctrine of vocation insisted that work must be service rendered to the neighbor and to the world.[329] Luther's concept of vocation invested significance and dignity in everyday work.[330]

Later Reformers and Puritans believed in a double calling: a general calling to individual salvation and a particular calling to work. Ryken lists many examples of calling to salvation: **1 Timothy 6:12; 1 Corinthians 1:9; 2 Thessalonians 2:13-14; 1 Peter 2:9; Colossians 3:15; and 1 Corinthians 1:2**.[331] The particular call involves serving neighbors with one's gifts.[332] The call to a specific religious task or office has ample scriptural support: **Isaiah 6:1-10; Amos 7:15; Numbers 18:1-7; 2 Timothy 1:11; Acts 16:10; Ephesians 4:11; and 1 Corinthians 12:28**.[333] According to the Anglican Church Dioceses of Sydney, the implication of **1 Corinthians 7:20** is that a Christian man or woman should remain in their secular estate and current occupation unless God calls them to "a distinct apostolic, prophetic, evangelistic or teaching task," which should not be entered into volitionally just because it may be seen as having a greater impact for salvation of others than one's current work.[334] All are called to share the Word and the gospel to others (**Matt. 28:19-20**), but some among Jesus' disciples are called to do this kind of work full-time. While on earth, Jesus "chose" certain individuals among a larger body of disciples to go out and preach (**Mark 1:17, 2:14, 3:13; Luke 10:1; John 15:16**)—not every beloved disciple was sent out. God clearly calls some to work in a career or task that is "specifically religious or church-related."[335] However, there has been much disagreement over the centuries as to whether God calls people to other kinds of work and occupations, typically labeled as secular.[336] Prior to the Reformation, people considered only those who left their everyday work and entered church or monastery work to have a calling from God or a vocation. The Reformation extended this concept of vocation to include all occupations and related activities.[337]

Referencing the Greek word for *calling*, *klēsis*, found in **1 Corinthians 7:20**, the Reformers, Luther and Calvin, were the first to use the Latin term *vocatio* and the German term *Beruf* to express men's everyday tasks and stations.[338] Luther interpreted *klēsis* as "one's outer status or occupation."[339] Paul says in **1 Corinthians 7:20**, "*Let each man remain in that condition in which he was called.*" The Reformers interpreted Paul's words as referring to one's external situation or condition, not one's inner spiritual life, and thus "new Christians should not abandon their family situations or occupations."[340] Some would say that this verse indicates, "Christians are to remain in the Christian life and that it has nothing to do with occupation," yet Ryken disagrees and says that the context shows that "Paul is raising the issue of how conversion should affect one's everyday life."[341] Gordon Fee comments in favor of Luther's understanding, "The call *to* Christ has created such a change in one's essential relationship (with God) that one does not need to seek change in other relationships (with people). These latter are transformed and given new meaning by the former."[342] Thus, for Luther, one did not need to leave his particular work upon receiving Christ to find work that would please God: "The order of stations in the earthy kingdom has been instituted by God himself as a way of seeing that the needs of humanity are met on a day-to-day basis."[343] Serving neighbor was, in essence, serving God and pleasing to Him. In conclusion, according to Lee Smith, the implications of verses **1 Corinthians 7:20** and **7:24** "are that every believer has a calling, not just those who are in vocational 'full-time Christian ministry' and that no calling is better or higher than another in the eyes of God."[344]

In opposition to Luther's interpretation of vocation, *klēsis*, as "signifying one's outer status or occupation,"[345] Richardson says *klēsis*, or calling, in the New Testament "means God's call to repentance and faith and to a life of fellowship and service in the Church."[346] To interpret calling in the way Luther does would mean that Paul used *klēsis* "in a sense used nowhere else in his or any other Greek writings."[347] Additionally, Richardson says that the Bible does not record a person ever being "called to an earthly profession or trade by God"; instead, those whom God calls are to work within the Church and thus they become Christian workers regardless of their secular occupation.[348] Richardson says that **1 Corinthians 7:20** "does not bid the Christian to remain in the secular 'calling' (e.g., that of a slave) in which he was when he became a believer but to remain faithful to the calling of God."[349] According to Ellul, "Jesus never calls upon anyone to work. On the contrary, he constantly takes the men he calls away from their work, e.g., Peter, James, Levi, the man in the parable who wants to try out his oxen, and so forth."[350] Barth agrees.[351] Ellul says, "The call of God...is always a summons to the specific service of God" such as a prophet or apostle or king.[352] Additionally, "He is called to serve God by some exceptional act and without even realizing that he is doing it in God's service, e.g. the king of Syria, the king of Assyria, or Cyrus."[353] Ellul denies that work is a vocation in the traditional sense of the word. For Ellul, work "offers the possibility of sustaining life, of upholding the world, and of a continuation of history. . . and this is

God's will. At this level then, if at this level alone, we have vocation. God calls us to work (of any kind) in order to keep going this world which he has not yet decided to stop and judge."[354] In summary, some exegetes believe Luther misinterpreted **1 Corinthians 7:20**, the main text used to support his concept of vocation;[355] however, Schuurman says that the key elements of vocation in the tradition of Luther and Calvin have "deep roots in the Bible" and need to be defended and renewed, though also reshaped in light of important criticisms.[356]

Luther's idea of vocation belongs more to his "wider theological logic than to his specific interpretation" of **1 Corinthians 7:17-24**,[357] and thus vocation is also expressed in the Bible through "the priesthood of all believers," through references to God's servants, and through providence, without using the term "calling." The base for Luther's doctrine of vocation lies strongly upon his theology of "the priesthood of all believers" in **1 Peter 2:9**. Luther's emphasis that all believers are priests unto God meant all Christians in all occupations held as high a spiritual office as a priest, bishop, or the pope.[358] Thus in God's eyes, there is no difference in status between laity and clergy, between secular and sacred jobs, for all workers are called to minister unto God.

Ryken believes that "the Bible supports the idea that ordinary occupations and tasks are something to which God calls people, even though the phraseology is not always specifically that of calling" and gives the following as examples: Moses as leader in **Exodus 3-4**, David as king in **Psalms 78:70-71**, Saul as king in **1 Samuel 15:17**, and Bezalel as craftsman and other occupations in **Exodus 31:1-6**.[359] William Placher says that **Colossians 3:23** "does not use the word 'call,' but it certainly invites Christians to think of any task as work done in the Lord's service."[360] According to Ryken, "An office or task does not have to be termed a calling in order to be regarded as such."[361]

God's providence lays the foundation for Luther's concept of vocation. Kathryn Kleinhans discusses how Luther wrote about God exercising divine authority in "two kingdoms," or in two main spheres: "God is at work through the gospel, offering forgiveness and new life, and God is at work through the law, bringing order to the world."[362] Thus, God considers the "secular" world as a domain for divine service, in which a person can participate "insofar as one serves the God-given neighbor."[363] God brings the answer to the prayer, "Give us this day our daily bread,"[364] providentially, in the form of humans working real jobs to provide, transport, and obtain food and other necessities of life.[365] In God's providence, He cares for the world through natural structures (such as the sun, moon, stars, laws of gravity, entropy, etc.) and through "the work of His human creatures."[366] God provides tangibly for the necessities of human life by bestowing upon people aptitudes and then guiding them into particular occupations in the world to ensure that He supplies society with food, clothing, shelter, family, friends, neighbors, economic resources, and stable government;[367] Ryken says these are also "callings from God."[368] In the Reformed concept of work as vocation, "God Himself carries on his creative activity in this world," and sustains creation, through the work that God calls people to do.[369] "God's providence is seen as the force that arranged circumstances in such a way that a person has a particular work. God also equips a person with the necessary talents and abilities to perform the work. In fact, the original Protestants made this one of the tests to know whether one was in the right calling."[370] Thus, daily work has spiritual significance and dignity as the worker partners with God "in God's creating and sustaining activity on earth,"[371] which includes caring for humanity according to God's providence.

From a historical and cultural context, until the mid-twentieth century, most people had a limited choice for a career,[372] which was usually given to them instead of chosen by them,[373] and they usually entered the occupation of their parents to maintain stability in society. In Paul's day, it appears some new Christians may have wanted to change their occupational status and other circumstances to serve the Lord better, but Luther insisted—upon the authority of Paul in **1 Corinthians 7:20**—that one did not have to leave their occupation to serve Christ in "a supposedly higher and more spiritual calling."[374] According to Pawson, "Provided that your job is not immoral or illegal, you are already in his calling; if He wants you to change jobs, He'll tell you."[375] If a change of work is necessary, people should not be motivated to change out of selfishness but by the leading of the Lord, and thus the worker should regard the new work as a calling of God as well. As a person matures in the Christian faith, he "may very well receive another calling to somewhere else."[376]

Calvin, like Luther, believed **1 Corinthians 7:20** encouraged Christians to be content with their station in life and not to be eager to change their work situation without proper reason.[377] However, Calvin had a more dynamic view and felt that it was appropriate to change vocations to utilize fully one's gifts and talents to serve others more effectively. The Puritans had a practical method for determining if a person was in the right calling—by checking "if God had clearly equipped him or her for the work" through gifts and talents and abilities.[378] The Puritans spoke of vocation in terms of gifts and service for church work and worldly work, yet Volf does not acknowledge this early historical aspect when presenting his "new" theology of work based on gifts for service instead of vocation.

Volf presents important critiques of Luther's concept of vocation.[379] Richard Higginson summarizes Volf's critiques into two main criticisms: First, Luther's vocation does not address the problem of human alienation or the dehumanizing ways people work, like assembly line work that is mindless and repetitive; Second, Luther's vocation is too static in requiring workers to remain in their occupation, normally throughout a lifetime.[380] In the first criticism, since many people hate their job, feel exploited, and are underpaid, they feel their work is dehumanizing and alienating, and therefore could not have originated from God as a calling.[381] Surveying thirty-one Protestant and Catholic congregations, Davidson and Caddell found that workers who had more benefits, such as full-time employment, job security, and higher pay, were more inclined to think of their work as a calling.[382] In the second criticism, Volf emphasizes that Paul was writing **1 Corinthians 7:20** in the context of crisis with the thought that Jesus could return very soon; therefore, under these conditions, Paul recommends being content in their occupation as slaves or in their singleness.[383] Considering the current mobile society where most people do not keep a single job for a lifetime and normally switch jobs multiple times, a new view of work is needed that remains true to the Bible and to the real world. Volf desires to replace the concept of vocation with the concept of charism, or gift, since he believes it is more in line with the New Testament.[384]

God Gives Abilities, Gifts, and Opportunities for Working

Ideally, work should utilize people's gifts and talents given by God, especially if they are in God's appointed work, though Scripture does not guarantee full use of gifts and talents in their work. During sometimes of life, there may not a real-world need for the gifts or work interests that people have. Sometimes people may not have the freedom to choose the kind of work they want to do; but out of necessity, they need to take a job that meets the current needs of society and pays their bills. Nevertheless, the needs of the world, a person's gifts and skills, and a person's truest desires can be guides to their God-given career.[385] For the Calvinists, people derive vocation from one's gifts that people are to use for the benefit of neighbors. Thus, finding a station in life where people can employ these gifts and talents for their neighbor's benefit should be a priority for a Christian.[386] According to Sayers, work should encompass "the full expression of the worker's faculties,...and [be] the medium in which he offers himself to God," and then "work is not, primarily, a thing one does to live, but the thing one lives to do."[387] Workers who use their God-given talents are more inclined to be passionate about their work. Furthermore, Sayers advocates the principle that "every man should do the work for which he is fitted by nature"[388] and not ask of employment "how much a week?" but "will it exercise my faculties to the utmost?"[389] Thus, Sayers emphasizes an integrated life: By utilizing the talents given by God, a "worker is called to serve God in his profession or trade—not outside it."[390] People will make their greatest contribution as they work in a field that "corresponds to the way God has designed [them]."[391]

Even though "nowhere in the New Testament does God send a special anointing on people for secular tasks"[392] and even though "the New Testament passages about gifts and their exercise are restricted to discussions of the church,"[393] many believe people can use these gifts in the real work world. For many years, Wagner believed that people were to use spiritual gifts within the context of the Body of Christ, or essentially the local church and its outreach programs. Now, however, he believes that people can use them in the marketplace.[394] Ed Silvoso explains that the spiritual gifts in **Mark 16:17-18** "primarily [apply] to ministry in the marketplace" since the "entire world, the totality of creation, must be the focus of the mission entrusted to us, not just a church building or a gathering of believers."[395] When all work done by Christians is work done for the Lord (Col. 3:23), then God's gifts are surely given for use in all kinds of workplace settings, in similar ways as they are used in a church.[396] Volf also "asserts that charisms (Spirit gifts) include more than ecclesiastical activities" and gives as examples the gift of evangelist (**Eph. 4:11**) and the gift of giving to the poor.[397] Volf reasons that the church is currently in the "age of the eschatological Spirit"; therefore, Spirit enablement for skillful work is the inheritance of all believers, which was only given occasionally in the Old Testament, as for Bezalel and David (**Ex. 31:2-3; 1 Chron. 28:11-12**).[398]

According to Hillman, the five-fold gifts of **Ephesians 4:11-13** do not apply only to full-time vocational ministers: "Nowhere does the scripture indicate that these gifts and callings are vocational. The five-fold gifts operate in the workplace to prepare God's people. We need to see all of these gifts and callings operational in the workplace."[399] Bill Hammon makes the following comparisons: apostles are like founders, prophets are like strategists, evangelists are like sales managers, teachers are like trainers, and pastors are like local business managers.[400] Some ministry leaders have been calling for a restoration of the apostolic and prophetic offices for today, with an emphasis on the need for marketplace apostles, whom Wagner characterizes as having "extraordinary authority" in comparison to others in the body of Christ.[401] Some ministry leaders would go as far as to say that societal transformation is limited in effectiveness until workplace apostles are set in place and properly recognized.[402] Yet, the Assemblies of God—representative of other Christian groups with similar views on this topic—builds a case and declares, "Since the New Testament does not provide guidance for the appointment of future apostles, such contemporary offices are not essential to the health and growth of the church nor its apostolic nature."[403] Many groups do not recognize contemporary offices of apostle and prophet of **Ephesians 4:11**; however, many would acknowledge that believers do "exercise the ministry function of apostles and prophets."[404] Most groups would not object to believers functioning as an apostle in the sense of establishing new churches or works in unreached areas, and most Pentecostals and Charismatics do not object to the ongoing gift of prophecy (**1 Cor. 14:1**), especially when it is used to encourage or comfort (**1 Cor. 14:3**).[405]

Volf is in favor of replacing the concept of work as a vocation with the concept of work as a charism, or gift.[406] A perceived weakness of Luther's concept of vocation is that working people find themselves trapped in the station or work they are in because it is their vocation, or calling from God. However, according to Kleinhans, Luther did not really say that people are trapped in their station of work and could never transition out but only that Christians did not need to leave their station in order to find a different station that would be pleasing to God because their current station can already be used to serve Him.[407] Thus, Luther's concept of vocation is not as static as some would think. In any case, by associating "calling" with gifts instead of a static occupation, there is no issue with changing jobs or careers since people can still use their gifts of the Spirit faithfully in accordance with their calling. Even when unemployed, people could still use their gifts to serve family, society, and volunteer groups.[408]

According to Hillman, the biggest temptation for a successful workplace minister is pride. Workers should never forget that "God gives us the skill, the intelligence, the resources, the energy, the drive and the opportunities to accomplish something."[409] **Deuteronomy 8:17** warns, *"You may say in your heart, 'My power and the strength of my hand made me this wealth,'"* but one should never forget that it is God who gives the power to produce wealth (**8:18**). If one prospers from the work of their hands, it is ultimately due to the blessing of the Lord (**Deut. 16:15, 24:19, 28:12; Ps. 90:17**).

"Almost one out of every twenty **Proverbs** between **10:1** and **22:6** deal with the problem of laziness or the virtue of diligence"

CHAPTER EIGHT
WORK ETHICS AND ATTITUDES

Laziness and Idleness are Sins

Scriptures are clear in stating that laziness and idleness are sins (**Eph. 4:28; 2 Thess. 3:10-13; Prov. 21:25**), and Christians have a responsibility to warn, rebuke, and instruct those who are unruly, idle, or lazy (**1 Thess. 5:14**). It was sinful or "folly" to be idle between daybreak and sunset.[410] According to Pawson, since laziness is a sin, "then unemployment is an evil and Christians should be fighting unemployment" since it is a "dehumanizing experience" for a person to be out of work who wants to work.[411] Almost one out of every twenty **Proverbs** between **10:1** and **22:6** deal with the problem of laziness or the virtue of diligence; eighteen **Proverbs** in all.[412] Some Scriptures that contrast those who are lazy and sluggards with those who are desirably diligent include **Proverbs 6:6-11, 10:4, 12:24, 12:27**, and **13:4**.

Diligence

Diligence and excellence should characterize a Christian's work. Writing in the first century in a culture where approximately sixty million people, or one-third of the population of the Roman Empire, were slaves,[413] the Apostle Paul references these servants or workers using the Greek word *douloi*. According to Richardson, "'Workers' is perhaps the best modern rendering of *douloi*, even though it does not carry with it the suggestion of being tied to one's occupation and to one's employer."[414] Paul writes:

> [Workers], *in all things obey those who are your masters on earth, not with external* [eye-pleasing] *service, as those who merely please men, but with sincerity of heart, fearing the Lord. Whatever you do, do your work heartily, as for the Lord rather than for men; knowing that from the Lord you will receive the reward of the inheritance. It is the Lord Christ whom you serve.* (**Col. 3:22-24**)

Paul reiterates this same message in the parallel passage of **Ephesians 6:5-8**. To Pawson, the worst job in the world is being a slave, "with no pay, no free time," "no hope of changing jobs" or "advancing their career."[415] Yet, Paul addresses them, and all workers, by exhorting them to work whole-heartily, because Jesus is their boss now. With ultimate respect for the Lord, Christians who work "whole-heartily" unto Him will be inevitably working with diligence and excellence.

With reference to working "*whole-heartily to the Lord*" in **Col. 3:23-24**, Andy Stanley says that from God's perspective, "What you do is not as important as how you do it."[416] Too often people are focusing on where they can work next and how much they can make there, but God is interested in how a person works in the job they currently have and whether they work whole-heartily and with diligence. Stanley asks a few probing questions, "What would it look like tomorrow if you went to work and for one day you decided to do your work for the Lord and not for [your human boss]? What would it look like if you did your work with all your heart for the Lord? What would you have to change?"[417] To get some specific thoughts in the minds of his listeners, Stanley poses further questions to help determine areas needed for change, "What wouldn't you say? What would you do? Where wouldn't you go? What would happen at lunch? What time would you get there? How quickly would you respond?"[418] Stanley advises people to pray for help in working hard today in whatever place they are and to pray for help in leaving the thought of a job promotion or a career change to God, for God will be pleased and bless a person who works whole-heartily and diligently unto Him.[419]

Paul says to workers, *"do not be an eye-pleaser"* (**Eph. 6:6; Col. 3:22**). Kirk says an eye-pleaser is one who gives "minimum performance, unless someone is watching."[420] Kirk exhorts, "Don't work hard only when your boss is watching and then slack off when she or he isn't looking. Work hard and with passion all the time, as if you're working for Christ."[421] Moreover, "the Ultimate Boss is always watching and that reality leads us to work in 'sincerity of heart,' not putting on a show for management, but genuinely working at the tasks set before us."[422] Paul affirms the value of work in God's sight and exhorts workers to work well because it is the right thing to do.[423] True character is shown in what people do when they think no one else is looking.[424] Furthermore, **Ecclesiastes 9:10** says, *"Whatever your hand finds to do, verily, do it with all your might"* and **2 Timothy 2:15** encourages workman to *"be diligent."* **Proverbs** indicates that diligence in work is a great virtue (**16:3; 23:4; 31:10-31**). Closely tied to diligence is excellence, for work done with diligence unto the Lord is often done with excellence.

Excellence

God does all things with excellence (**Gen. 1-2; Ps. 8; Ps. 150:2**) and it matters to Him that people also do their work with excellence (**Col. 3:23-24; Eccles. 9:10; Heb. 11:4; 1 Cor. 12:31; Prov. 22:29; Dan. 6:3**). The Bible describes Bezalel in **Exodus 31:1-6** as a man filled with the Spirit of God who did excellent work for God. In the same manner, Christians ought to do all their work with excellence as the Spirit of God certainly resides and operates in them. Daniel and his friends also did work with excellence to such an extent that the king exclaimed that they were ten times better than all others were (**Dan. 1:19-20**). Daniel had distinguished himself with exceptional qualities and attitudes, yet he would not compromise with idolatry (**Dan. 6:1-3**). Joseph was an excellent worker with a great attitude, yet he would not compromise with immorality, and God promoted him. An excellent attitude is desired (**1 Cor. 10:31; Col. 3:23-24**). Excellence takes hard work.

Hillman makes a good point in *The 9 to 5 Window* of why it is necessary to work with excellence in serving others:

> *One of the easiest ways to discredit Christ in the workplace is for Christians to do inferior work. In order to earn respect, our work should stand apart because we do our work unto the Lord (see **Col. 3:17**). Doing quality work will not be the primary means of winning others to Christ, but doing poor-quality work can disqualify us very quickly from ever having the opportunity to present Christ in a positive light.*[425]

"Work well done, whether that of rulers or that of slaves, is service rendered to God; and this is true of the work of Christians and non-Christians alike. The difference between the two is that Christians are aware of this truth, and they will accordingly strive to work more diligently and more faithfully—'as unto the Lord.'"[426] The Lord himself will reward workers with an inheritance in His new creation when they work faithfully and passionately unto Him (**Col. 3:24**) with excellence. Joy can fill workers when they sense and know that they are serving Christ.

Contentment and Joy

God can redeem work for the Christian and change it from drudgery to joy. "When a man turns to Christ in repentance and faith, his whole life is sanctified, including his life as a worker. What had formerly been done as sheer necessity, or perhaps out of a sense of duty, or even as a means of self-expression and fulfillment, is now done "unto the Lord", and becomes joyous and free service and the source of deep satisfaction."[427] Scriptures say that a Christian should be joyful in all circumstances of life (**Phil. 4:4**) including their work (**Eccles. 3:22**).

From a basis of joy, Christians strengthened by Christ can be content with their work— instead of complaining—by imitating the attitude exhibited by Paul (**Phil. 4:11-12**) and by not striving for an abundance of wealth (**2 Tim. 6:6-8; Prov. 23:4**). Often people look to Hollywood, TV, Fortune 500 companies, or an ideal person and wish they could do a similar kind of "significant work" instead of the kind of work they are doing currently. Recognizing one's vocation, or call of God to a work or task, helps a person accept the drudgery of one's work or task more easily, and it even gives them a sense of importance, or joy, knowing that God values their kind of work. Acknowledging God's providence, the Reformers stressed that Scripture encourages contentment in one's work arena in which one has been called by God (**1 Cor. 7:20**) as all legitimate work can be done unto Christ. If God wants to change a person's work, God can lead and guide that person as such. In addition, while it is important to have goals in work-life, Lee Smith says, contentment comes as people "realize that none of us ever accomplishes all that we desire and then accept that reality."[428] People can and should take pleasure in a job well done and take joy in their accomplishments from working.[429]

Submissive, Faithful, Trustworthy, Respectful, and not Argumentative to Bosses

Workers are to be submissive and obedient to their bosses (**Col. 3:22; Titus 2:9; 1 Pet. 2:18-25**), faithful to their assignments (**Prov. 25:13**), trustworthy (**1 Cor. 4:2**) and honest—not one to steal (**Titus 2:10**), respectful of their bosses (**1 Tim. 6:1-2**) and not argumentative with them (**Titus 2:9**). Kirk describes an obedient worker as one who exhibits a "can do" attitude even when given a tough responsibility.[430] While not approving of slavery, Paul reminds Christians that they will receive a permanent reward from Jesus if they are working for His glory (**Col. 3:24**). The difficulties that a Christian experiences in work during their brief time on earth will be eclipsed by their eternal reward to come (**Col. 3:24; Eph. 6:8; 1 Cor. 3:11-15**).[431]

Fair and Just toward Employees

Scripture opposes employers who "*oppress the wage earner in his wages*" (**Mal. 3:5**). Samuel J. Schultz comments on these "defrauders" saying, "They were people who cheated hired workers by paying less than the agreed-upon wage, or by paying a nonliving wage to people who were so desperate that they would work for any price."[432] Employers were not to delay payment to workers, but were to pay on schedule as expected so that the employees could buy their daily necessities (**Lev. 19:13; Deut. 24:14-15; James 5:4**). Even the Apostle Paul took issue with the Corinthian church for not providing material compensation for his spiritual ministry to them, yet all workers are worthy of compensation (**1 Cor. 9:6-12**). Jesus said, a "*laborer is worthy of his wages*" (**Luke 10:7**), and thus employers are to give a fair wage to their workers (**Col. 4:1**) and treat their employees justly (**Col. 4:1; Eph. 6:9**) and in the same way they would like to be treated, for employers have a boss in heaven as a follower of Jesus (**Eph. 6:9**).

CHAPTER NINE
BALANCING WORK AND OTHER SIGNIFICANT PRIORITIES

Balancing Work and Other Significant Priorities

A workaholic is a person who works too much, perhaps compulsively, and often sees leisure as unnecessary. Determining if one is working too much varies according to cultures and situations. However, people should consider the number of hours that they work against the negative effects of long hours (see Table 1) and the neglect of other necessary priorities. Although a forty-hour workweek may be a norm in today's society, in an agrarian economy during Biblical times, six days of work could equate to an eighty-hour week.[433] According to Mahaney, workaholics "neglect the more important matters and priorities such as family, relationships, [and] involvement in the church."[434] For some, work has become an idol. John A. Bernbaum and Simon M. Steer explain this further:

> Scripture often defines such idolatry as an excessive concern for acquiring material possessions. The vanity of accumulating wealth (see **Eccles. 2:4-11; 5:10**) is a manifestation of idolizing work. In our own day this aspect of idolatry is coupled with the assessment of a person's

> *social status on the basis of that person's job. This in turn cultivates attitudes of pride, envy, and insecurity.*[435]

Work in moderation is a good thing, but it can become idolatrous when a person trusts more in their work to sustain themselves than in God and when work is the only thing that encompasses a person's life and identity.

People often ask a new acquaintance the question "What do you do for a living?" In Western culture in particular, this common question shows the priority and preoccupation people have with a person's job or career: "one's profession has become a primary criteria for assessing the worth and value of an individual. 'You are what you do' is a common phrase...This is not a biblical criteria for personal value or worth."[436] Yet many people feel prideful or worthless depending upon the kind of work they do and how society values that kind of work. In some areas, people look down on a homemaker or a stay-at-home mom in comparison to one who is an important professional who makes money. For others, if they lose their job, they feel they have no value anymore and do not know who they are—they have drawn their identity and security from what they do. Mahaney explains where people should find their identity:

> *We find our identity as Christians and our security in the character of God and the person of Jesus Christ and His finished work on our behalf. We find our identity and security in the fact that we have been made in the image of God...that we have been relationally reconciled to God through what Jesus Christ has done on our behalf on the cross.*[437]

For Pawson, a Christian should find their identity in being a child of God by adoption.[438]

The highest value in life should be a person's relationship with God and the identity this gives them in being God's children and new creatures in Christ.[439] According to Ryken, the most important thing in life is not work but faithfulness to God.[440] God is to be our master, not our work or money (**Matt. 6:24**). **Matthew 6:33** says to "*seek first His Kingdom and His righteousness.*" According to Lee Smith:

> *If our work gets between us and our relationship with God, our relationship with our spouse and children, or our willingness to serve Christ and His church, it has become an idol. This is a constant temptation many people face, since traditionally hard work has been commended in the Christian community. Knowing where the line is between diligence and an idolatrous compulsion to work is not always easy to distinguish.*[441]

However, Mahaney says it is possible to pursue excellence in a career and "have a profession without it becoming an obsession." To accomplish this, people need balance in life.

To implement a balanced life, Pat Gelsinger advises people to set a personal mission statement based on one's values and suggests that the highest value or priority should be God, followed by family, followed by one's work.[442] Similarly, Ted W. Engstrom and David J. Juroe give three broad levels of priorities: first, commitment to God in Christ; second, commitment to the Body of Christ—the church, encompassing possibly a spouse, then immediate family, then extended family; and third, commitment to work in the world.[443] With these priorities as a basis, to get out of the "work trap," they say that goals need to be set (or readjusted), such as reading God's Word and praying, spending quality time with family, spending time in church, spending time in leisure, serving others in some kind of need, planning goals each week, and serving diligently at one's job.[444] A workaholic often misses, or simply does not enjoy, special moments that cannot be repeated—celebrating an anniversary, a birth, a birthday, a child's baseball game, etc.—but "one of the special privileges in life is spending precious moments with those who love us dearly, our spouses, children, close friends."[445]

Rest and Leisure

God Himself rested after working six days (**Gen. 2:2**), thus forming an example for man to follow (**Ex. 20:11**). The fourth commandment says to *"Remember the Sabbath day, to keep it holy"* (**Ex. 20:8**) and not do any work on that day (**Ex. 20:10**) but *"rest"* (**Deut. 5:14**). Additionally,

Ryken says that God rested after each individual day of creation, as He "contemplated and (we infer) enjoyed what he had created, pronouncing it 'good.'"[446] God has given humankind regular rhythms of work/rest: working during the day and resting at night; working six days of the week and having a Sabbath rest on the seventh, to recuperate one's body and mind and to realign with the Creator and His Creation.[447] After working hard during the day, rest from work is needed to regain energy and alertness, to be able to work hard and well during the next day, and so on. A full day off from work, or a short vacation, could also replenish a person to be ready and able to continue working hard and well. In the Old Testament, God had also given other rest days for annual feasts. Rest from work is different from leisure.

Leisure, according to Ryken, encompasses three aspects: "time free from constraints of obligation or necessity"; activities regarded as leisure; and a sense of satisfaction, enrichment, or celebration.[448] Mackenzie and Kirkland distinguish between rest and leisure saying that rest is the biblical opposite of work, whereas leisure "has as its goal personal enjoyment—which may well be a by-product of rest, but not its purpose."[449] For example, one may visit theme parks in one's leisure and have fun and yet not be rested by the activities. Restful activities are necessary and may include such things as reading, walking, praying, or gardening; but there is nothing wrong with enjoying leisure activities in moderation. According to Ryken, "The accounts that the Bible gives us of God's creation of the world and Jesus' life and personality suggest that God is playful as well as serious. And if he made a world in which Wisdom and Leviathan can play [**Prov. 8:30-31; Ps. 104:26**], his human creatures may do the same."[450]

Sayers observes that people too often try to rush through their workday or workweek in anticipation of their leisure, yet leisure should be looked upon "as the period of changed rhythm that refresh[es] us for the delightful purpose of getting on with our work."[451] Richardson says, "The hours of daylight were the hours of labour for all workers (cf. **Ps. 104:22f.; John 9:4**), whose only leisure-time was during the hours of darkness. The general standpoint of the Bible is that it is 'folly' (i.e., sinful) to be idle between daybreak and sunset. A six- or an eight-hour day was not [envisioned]," thus, Richardson says not much guidance is given in the Bible on how to use leisure;[452] yet, Ryken disagrees with that and reasons from the Bible for leisure.[453] Rest will also be a facet of eternal life (**Rev. 14:13**).

Retirement

Retiring from paid work is especially acceptable for older people who are no longer able to perform adequately the duties of one's paid work—in which case it is ethically appropriate to retire. Rayburn says **Ecclesiastes 12:1-5** gives a realistic description of old age and its consequences and uses **1 Timothy 5:4** to show that there are stages of life, with an implication that retirement is one of those stages where parents no longer have paid employment.[454] Retirement should not result in idleness. Mahaney suggests looking at retired people who are idle to discover that most of them are miserable people because they are defying the way that God has made them.[455] Retirement should not be for the purpose of self-indulgence or play, for this is difficult to justify biblically, but retirement may properly produce self-fulfillment.[456] Retirement should enable one the freedom for other kinds of service. Regardless of whether one works for money or not, or is retired, one should always be serving God and people, as an appropriate obligation, for as long as one is physically and mentally able. Thus, while it is acceptable to retire from work, including vocational ministry, God does not permit a person to retire from serving Christ and His people, for Christ's sake.[457]

Although the Bible does not speak of an age in which to retire, there is one exception to this given to the Levites and priests to retire from their particular functions at the age of fifty (**Num. 4:3, 23; 8:25**), maybe because of physical strength limitations. The implication from these verses is that there may be appropriate age limits set for some kinds of work, like pilots, due to physical or mental limitations that come with old age. Thus, while it may be permissible for some companies to insist on retirement at a particular age for appropriate reasons, for a person who is willing and able to perform one's work functions, there is no biblical requirement for mandatory retirement at a particular age. The great old Testament characters (e.g. Moses, Joseph, and David) were most productive in their later years life, and God can use all willing and able people until the end of their lives, as they use their gifts in a variety of new ways, laboring with God and possibly pouring into young people.[458] Once retired, a completely new world of enjoyable service begins.

"Even before the Fall, God gave man work to do in having dominion over creation"

CHAPTER TEN
CHRISTIAN MODELS FOR UNDERSTANDING THE MEANING OF WORK

Vocational, Trinitarian, Charismatic, Ontological, and Collaborative Models

Robert Barnett has identified several complementary models that summarize a theology of work. In the Lutheran Vocational Model, God providentially cares for humanity by placing people in a particular vocation throughout society to serve one another with their talents. In the Reformed Vocational Model, people see God as providentially caring for creation through each person's work but work also involves a worshipful attitude and a context for sanctification where work transforms the worker. In the Trinitarian Model, scholars use the work of each person of the Trinity as an analogy of how God desires humans to do their work. For example, the Trinity engages in distinctive personal work, cooperative work, egalitarian work, and self-giving and loving work. In the Charismatic Model, scholars place the emphasis on work that uses one's *Charisma*, or spiritual gifts, talents, and abilities, to accomplish God's purposes of transforming culture. In the Ontological Model, work is seen as an end in itself since it has value to a God who Himself is a worker, and work is also seen as an instrumental means to an end in providing money for the worker and services to society along with personal fulfillment. In the Roman Catholic Collaborative Model, people see all work as having some measure of toil and difficulty. Further, work has an objective meaning in which ordinary activities and work contribute to God's work, and work has a subjective meaning in which men and women can realize their humanity.[459]

Penitential, Creationist, and Eschatological Approach

Charles Ringma gives the three approaches to a theology of work identified by the French Jesuit, Joseph Thomas: the penitential, the creationist, and the eschatological.[460] For the penitential, work is a curse for original sin and seen as persistent suffering for which the worker must endure. For the creationist, work is seen as the result of the Genesis mandate to subdue the earth (**Gen 1:26-28**) and to cultivate and care for it (**Gen. 2:15**). "Man's work is thus seen as cooperation with God in the continuing act of creation and dominating matter."[461] In the eschatological, work is seen as "the outpouring of human activity in the journey towards God's final kingdom."[462] Moreover, people "see a direct link between this world and the world to come" and thus some work will have "an echo" in the world to come.[463]

Theology of Creation, Anthropology, and Incarnation

A good Christian theology of work emphasizes key theological categories, according to James M. Roseman, and must rest on a "three-legged stool": the theology of creation, the theology of anthropology, and the theology of the Incarnation.[464] A theology of creation views God as a worker in **Genesis 1-2** and creates man to work and have dominion over creation. Even before the Fall, God gave man work to do in having dominion over creation and in being a steward over the limited earthly resources to meet the needs of people. God continues to work by sustaining creation, and people participate through their own work in God's continuing work. A theology of anthropology emphasizes the *Imago Dei*, or the Image of God in man (**Gen. 1:26-27**), and the common nature to work. In the theology of the Incarnation, emphasis is on showing the significance of God taking on human form (**John 1:14**), which shows God's positive view of the material realm and His intent to redeem all of creation and not just immaterial souls and thus people should work toward the transformation of creation.[465]

The "Integration Box" Model

David Miller found that there are four different ways to integrate faith and work, which he calls the "Integration Box" model or framework, consisting of the Four E's: ethics, evangelism, experience, and enrichment.[466] Miller summarizes these: Ethics, where faith is used as a moral foundation and as a source of guidance for ethical issues; Experience, where work takes on intrinsic meaning and purpose as it is seen as a calling; Enrichment, where spiritual disciplines help ground a person in their stressful work situations using prayer or devotionals for encouragement; Evangelism, where witnessing to others in the workplace is emphasized in accordance with the Great Commission (**Matt. 28:19-20**).[467] Miller's four categories illustrate the main approaches taken by different individuals and groups within the Faith at Work movement.[468]

PART 4
FAITH AT WORK MOVEMENT

"...every believer being a minister in every place all the time"

Pete Hammond

CHAPTER ELEVEN
BACKGROUND OF FAITH AT WORK MOVEMENT

Defining the Faith at Work Movement

The Faith at Work movement is predominantly Christian-based and helps "people integrate the claims of their faith with the demands of their work."[469] People incorporate practically different aspects of a theology of work in the movement as a whole. Some leaders within the movement emphasize work as a divine calling to ministry, others emphasize the Great Commission of witnessing and making disciples (**Matt. 28:18-20**), others emphasize the Creation Mandate to care for God's creation (**Gen. 1:26**), others emphasize the intrinsic value of everyday work (**Col. 3:12**), and others emphasize economic justice for the oppressed (**Deut. 24:14-15**).[470] From a broader perspective, the movement emphasizes "activity around the issue of every believer being a minister in every place all the time," which includes witnessing and serving others in word and deed in the workplace as well as working with excellence unto Christ for the glory of God.[471]

Some people may know the Faith at Work movement by various other names such as Marketplace movement, Marketplace Ministry, Workplace Ministry, Ministry in Daily Life, Work-Life Ministry, and Faith and Work movement. Some other names emphasizing spirituality have been used such as Workplace Spirituality, Spirituality at Work, Spirituality of Work, and Spirituality in the Workplace; however, the Workplace Spirituality movement that has bloomed since the late 1990s normally uses these terms and it incorporates a broader faith perspective than just Christianity. Yet, even though Miller focuses only on Christianity in his book *God at Work*, he sees the Faith at Work movement as "highly diverse, comprising nearly all of the major religions"[472] and "those who reject organized religion altogether, preferring to pick and choose from various religious traditions."[473] Miller has this broad view by placing the Workplace Spirituality movement under a Faith at Work umbrella, yet other authors of both camps do not. Nancy Smith, author of *Workplace Spirituality*, agrees with the distinction of the two saying the Faith at Work movement is "focused on the Christian faith"[474] while the Workplace Spirituality movement values "spiritual diversity at work"[475] and "looks to the morality and ethics that are common to most of the world's religions."[476] Smith describes an ideal vision of Workplace Spirituality as "a workplace where everyone feels safe and free to practice their own faith whether through prayer, meditation, dietary rules or clothing and where each person's unique spirituality is honored as an asset to the workplace."[477]

In contrast, the Faith at Work movement focuses on integrating one's Christian faith with one's work, yet the movement is very diverse within Christianity. The movement includes a "loose network of individuals and groups" of men and women of all corporate levels in all types of work, as well as conferences, e-newsletters, websites, books, magazines, podcasts, and radio shows.[478] According to Hammond, the activity of the movement "is very broad and diverse, cutting across the whole spectrum of God's people in North America (and now internationally too), from Roman Catholics, to Orthodox, to Mainline Protestants, to Evangelicals, to Charismatics and in independent congregations."[479]

The *2003 – 2004 International Faith and Work Directory* is a resource for the Faith at Work movement that "provides a 'snapshot' of the movement with a comprehensive list of individuals, companies, agencies, organizations, groups and networks that are dedicated to serving God's people in the workplace."[480] At the time of its publication, it listed 1,200 organizations in the directory, the vast majority of which were non-profit workplace ministries. In 2004, the Directory grew to contain more than 1,400 listings, of which more than 900 were non-profit national or international workplace ministries.[481] The movement's growth is also seen by examining the number of books published on the "faith-workplace connection," which according to a statement from Pete Hammond has grown from 350 titles to 2000 titles from the years 2000 to 2005, thus indicating a "move of God" and growth in the Faith at Work movement.[482] In addition, local churches are starting to be equipped to focus on faith at work issues, and there is a great need for this. As Hillman recognizes, "people are hungry to know how to effectively integrate their faith life with their work life, and they are energized by the call."[483]

Historical Progression of Faith at Work Movement

Historically astute individuals credit two organizations as being pioneers in the Faith at Work movement. According to Wagner, the historical starting point should be in 1930 when several individuals formed Christian Business Men's Committee (**CBMC**).[484] While being a non-charismatic evangelical marketplace ministry, CBMC also attracted some Charismatics and Pentecostals, including Demos Shakarian in 1942, who then promptly founded the Downey, California group and served as its president for the first two years.[485] Although Demos felt that CBMC had good men who "loved Jesus," he desired to have more "spirit or fire in the meetings."[486] "Usually the Pentecostals, out of respect for the ecumenical nature of the organization were forced to mute their spirituality and refrain from praying for the sick or manifesting such gifts of the Spirit as prophecy and speaking in tongues."[487] Demos placed most of his efforts into organizing and funding crusades with Pentecostals evangelists, yet at the same time, he was "a faithful member of the Downey CBMC chapter" where he "learned much about how to organize and run a local chapter of this type of organization."[488]

According to Hillman, "The faith at work movement has its early beginnings in the 1950s when the [interdenominational organization]

Full Gospel Businessmen's Fellowship International [**FGBMFI**] was birthed through Demos Shakarian. This was a group of enthusiastic and passionate business men birthed from the Charismatic renewal movement in the '50s and '60s."[489] Both CBMC and FGBMFI used a similar format of a mealtime evangelistic meeting where a fellow businessman shares a testimony of how he came to know Jesus and the difference that Jesus has made in his life.[490] According to Hillman, "These two organizations represent the focus of workplace ministries [since the 1950's]. That focus has largely been on executives [and professionals], men, and evangelism. These ministries were also birthed outside the local church and have often been seen by church leaders as competition to the local church."[491] For example, although "many Assemblies of God adherents shared the excitement and vision that prompted efforts like the FGBMFI," "some local pastors disliked the time and money their well-to-do business members devoted to the FGBMFI."[492] Because Demos Shakarian emphasized at every meeting that members should be active in their church and pay tithes to their home church, Shakarian states, "Those who attended our meetings invariably became the hardest workers and biggest givers of their home congregations. But still churches eyed the Fellowship with suspicion."[493] CBMC addressed the "anti-church charge" with a poll of its membership that showed that 100% of CBMC's members were also active members of their church and 67% were teachers or leaders of their church's Sunday Schools.[494] "Both CBMC and FGBMFI acknowledged a high esteem for the local church. Most of the leaders were church members."[495] Yet, both groups felt that businesspeople would be more effective in evangelizing the marketplace and initially following-up on its fruit than the pastors, thus church leaders often saw CBMC and FGBMFI as "competitors of the local churches."[496] Initially, FGBMFI stimulated fellowship primarily among Pentecostals, but by the late 1950s, meetings drew many non-Pentecostal church people, many of whom then received the Baptism in the Holy Spirit, and FGBMFI became a catalyst to the worldwide Neo-Pentecostal, or Charismatic, movement.[497] "Although it was stressed that FGBMFI was not a replacement for the local church, many pastors felt threatened by this open ecumenical fellowship."[498] They were "concerned over the ultimate threat of a possible new denomination issuing from the dynamically growing group" in spite of statements from FGFMFI leadership of their desire to work with "believing churches" and not be a substitute for them or any denomination or men's group.[499] FGBMFI has had phenomenal success worldwide and has effectively evangelized working people. During the past few decades, many other significant workplace ministries were springing up and reaching out, including FCCI and ICCC in the 1980s, but the Faith at Work movement "is largely a phenomenon of the 1990s" that began to soar in the late 1990s, with a "tipping point" occurring "around 1997 or 1998."[500]

The existence of the Faith at Work movement was "affirmed" by the July 9, 2001 issue of Fortune magazine, with their cover story titled "God and Business" that states that believers "want to bridge the traditional divide between spirituality and work."[501] Wagner says many Christian workplace leaders considered this a "watershed event," coming across "as a de facto, cultural stamp of approval on [the] movement."[502] "Major secular media" have covered many other stories describing this trend and Christian media since 2004, including an article in the *New York Times Magazine* on October 31, 2004, that features a cover story on Christianity in the workplace entitled "With God at Our Desks."[503]

"Evangelism is not an end goal of workplace ministry; it is the fruit"

Os Hillman

CHAPTER TWELVE
PROFILES OF DIFFERENT ORGANIZATIONS

The Founding and Leadership of Different Organizations

Multiple ministry organizations that specialize on the marketplace have formed and expanded over the years. Some of the most prominent of these ministries include:

- **CBMC** founded in 1930 by a small group of Christian businessmen and whose current president is David Meyers, as of 2020

- **FGBMFI** founded in 1952 by Demos Shakarian and whose current president is Mario Garcia Olvera, as of 2018

- **Executive Ministries** founded in the early 1960s by Arthur DeMoss as a ministry of Campus Crusade for Christ, and now merged into another a ministry of CRU

- **FCCI** founded in 1977 by Bobby Mitchell and others, and whose current president is Lee Truax, as of 2019

- **ICCC** founded in 1985 by Swedish businessman Gunnar Olson

- **C12 Group** founded in 1992 by Buck Jacobs and whose current president is Mike Sharrow

- **CMDL** founded in 1991 by Lutherans Bill Diehl and Sally Simmel, though ended in 2011
- **Marketplace Leaders** founded in 1996 by Os Hillman, who serves as its president

While some of the smaller Faith at Work ministries may only sponsor events, many consider each of these larger ministries listed as Fellowships.

Mission and Background of Different Organizations

CBMC

Christian Business Men's Connection (CBMC) was founded under the name of Christian Business Men's **Committee** (CBMC) in Chicago in 1930. The term "committee" was originally used to emphasize that each member should be part of a group and perform specific duties.[504] This organization ministers to all levels of businesspeople and professionals through events such as luncheons and small-group Bible studies. From their web site, "Christian Business Men's Connection is a global men's ministry, founded during the Great Depression, that equips business and professional men to lead well, impact their communities and engage The Great Commission. Today, men are experiencing authentic relationships that result in Christ-led business and Christ-centered families."[505] CBMC has a two fold mission, "to present Jesus Christ as Savior and Lord to business and professional men and to develop Christian business and professional men to carry out the Great Commission."[506] In addition to an emphasis on sharing the gospel via evangelism, CBMC emphasizes making disciples using the Word of God via Operation Timothy (OT), where a mentor ("a Paul") personally assists a learner ("a Timothy") in a transformational journey of exploring Christ's Word.

Since its beginning in 1930, CBMC has grown considerably. In 1937, several similar groups within the USA linked together under the acronym CBMC, and thus Christian Business Men's Committee

International came into existence, with its Support Center in Chicago.[507] In 1938, the first CBMC International Conference was held in Chicago with five committees, and a five-person steering committee was formed, with Ben Hedstrom becoming the first chairman of CBMC. The organization became international by 1941 with the establishment of committees in London and Ontario, Canada.[508] By 1947, there were 162 CBMC groups, primarily throughout the USA and Canada,[509] and by 1962, there were more than 500 committee groups[510] with a total of 15,000 members (about 30 per group) in 35 countries.[511] In the 1970s, the ministry moved its Administrative Center from Chicago to Chattanooga. Robert Tamasy gives an open assessment of their growing pains: "Over time, beginning around 1975, many countries had broken from the single CBMC Board and had become independent with their own boards of directors [to better deal with linguistic and cultural differences]. Many had lost any emphasis on evangelism and discipleship, turning into congenial fellowship groups with no outward ministry focus."[512] CBMC looked different in each country with no commonality of mission or strategy. To help with this, in 1987, CBMC International was newly incorporated as the Global Association for CBMC National associations, reorganizing the "loose confederation" of 21 independent CBMC national ministries around a new constitution and bylaws and formalized guidelines "for evangelizing and discipling business and professional people."[513] Roger Erickson was chosen as the new CBMC International President, serving in that role for ten years until 1997.[514] Further in 1987, a distinction was made between CBMC (proper), representing the large USA organization of CBMC groups (or "teams"), and CBMC International, encompassing a global oversight of all other nations having CBMC teams, with the USA organization providing strong support and cooperation. The two organizations have two different web sites: The web site for USA-based CBMC is www.cbmc.com, and the web site for CBMC International is www.cbmcint.com.

In the 1990s, and definitely by 2005, CBMC (in the USA) officially changed its name to *Christian Business Men's **Connection***, to emphasize not only connections for people in building business and seeking jobs, but to emphasize their calling to *connect* men with God, to *connect* men with other men to share the gospel, and to *connect* men with other men to help in their spiritual growth.[515] Yet, other national CBMC associations like using the CBMC acronym for the name *Connecting Business and Marketplace to Christ*, thus removing its "men-only" emphasis and stating its purpose is to connect "*all*" business leaders and professionals to Christ.[516] Further, CBMC International does not define the name for the CBMC acronym in its Ministry Reports or on its International web site with the exception of its Donation page, where it also uses the name *Connecting Business and Marketplace to Christ*.[517] In the 2016 and 2018 CBMC International Ministry Report, ladies from different nations are seen and described as joining CBMC International, and the report defines the organization's participants as follows, "CBMC International is a global association of Christian business and professional men **and women** devoted to living and sharing the Gospel of Jesus Christ in the workplace"; and the ministry practice of "Teams" is described as "Effective teams of business and professional men **and women** who support one another and share our gifts in the marketplace."[518] Thus, CBMC International, as the global network of CBMC national associations, encourages participation of both men and women without the historical emphasis of men-only, and thus it seems national associations have the freedom to go in either direction based on culture and direction of national leadership.

CBMC and its sister organization, CBMC International, have had remarkable growth since their beginning in 1930. Bill McAvinney, CBMC President (2017–2020), stated that in 2019, CBMC in the USA had 557 teams located in 338 cities (a 25% increase over 2018), and they hosted 524 events with 60,574 in attendance in total.[519] The CBMC web site (in 2007) documented that CBMC International was active in over 70 countries with over 50,000 members in total, with about one-third of the members in the USA.[520] As of 2018, CBMC International is "reaching business and professional people in more than 80 nations,"[521] and the 2018 CBMC International Ministry Report states it is touching 94 nations in 6 continents: "CBMC International is an interdenominational, evangelical Christian organization comprised of 94 national associations around the world. We share a common statement of beliefs, ministry practices and a passion to see lives transformed by the Gospel of Jesus Christ."[522] An organization similar in structure and growth to CBMC International is FGBMFI.

FGBMFI

Full Gospel Business Men's Fellowship International (FGBMFI) is an interdenominational organization founded in 1952 by a successful California dairyman and real estate developer, Demos Shakarian. He and his father owned the largest dairy in the world in the 1940's. In the midst of this business success, Demos' desire was to reach men in all nations for Jesus Christ, especially those in the marketplace. The personal story of Demos Shakarian along with the phenomenal story of the birth and growth of FGBMFI is vividly recorded in the book, *The Happiest People on Earth*. First published in 1975, this book sold over one million copies in twenty-five languages by 1990.[523] Lee Braxton, a very successful businessman and one of the original five directors of FGBMFI in 1952, provided an impetus for the new organization in their first published *Voice* magazine, stating: "Business and professional men are needed to help extend Christ's kingdom. Too long many of us have been busy making our own success in life, and in many cases we have not been given the opportunity to serve our church or the cause of Christianity in the way we could serve best, and we hope to do this through the Fellowship."[524] From its founding in the early 1950's, FGBMFI has made a huge impact on the spiritual lives of people in the USA and around the world. Remarkably in the late 1980s, the Fellowship had grown to a worldwide attendance at monthly outreach meetings exceeding one million persons, with half of that in the USA. Further, it was reaching 117 nations with more than 3,000 chapters, of which 1,700 chapters were active in the United States with 45,000 participating members.[525]

FGBMFI chapters of men usually meet on a monthly or weekly basis to host dinner, lunch, or breakfast meetings for fellowship, ministry, and outreach, with a focus primarily on evangelization, usually through the sharing of testimonies. Demos Shakarian considered each word in the name of the FGBMFI organization as important to describing its function and focus:

> *Full Gospel*. That meant no subject would have to be avoided at our meetings. Healing. Tongues. Deliverance.

Whatever the man's experience, he could talk about it, just as it happened.

Business Men. Laymen. Ordinary people.

Fellowship. That's what it should feel like. A bunch of people who love to get together—not a rules and committees and meeting-come-to-order kind of thing.

International...The whole world. All flesh.[526]

While possibly coincidental, the new name seems to have derivatives from the "CBMC International" name. Demos was very familiar with the name and organization of "Christian Business Men's Committee International" and yet wanted to have an organization focused on a specific group of Christians—**Full Gospel** Christians—and he wanted to NOT use the word "Committee" (with its connotations) to describe the group but wanted to emphasize a warmer, loving "**Fellowship**" group. Thus, in the end, he had essentially substituted:

- "Full Gospel" for "Christian"
- "Fellowship" for "Committee"

thus, deriving **Full Gospel** *Business Men's* **Fellowship** *International*. Although "the first generation of leaders were upscale Pentecostal businessmen, much like the founder, Demos Shakarian," and membership was "mostly made up of business or professional men, there were always thousands of men who were everyday farmers and laborers",[527] in all spheres of work. Furthermore, "Despite the words 'Business Men' in its name, the Fellowship accepted any man who desired to belong as long as he accepted the beliefs and practices of the organization,"[528] which are based on the "Articles of Faith" of the "Pentecostal Fellowship of North America (PFNA)."[529] On the FGBMFI website, the mission of the FGBMFI is given:

1. *To reach men in all nations for Jesus Christ*
2. *To call men back to God*

3. *To help believers to be baptized in the Holy Spirit and to grow spiritually*

4. *To train and equip men to fulfill the Great Commission*

5. *To provide an opportunity for Christian fellowship*

6. *To bring greater unity among all people in the body of Christ.*[530]

The Fellowship exhibits a prime emphasis upon evangelism. In chapter meetings and conventions, the Fellowship encourages faith and an atmosphere in which prophetic ministry, miracles, healings, signs and wonders can take place. Speakers at meetings often testify of God's amazing and miraculous intervention in their lives and businesses. There is a renewed emphasis that encourages the "full gospel" in the meetings of the Full Gospel Business Men's Fellowship International.

Serving as International Secretary for FGBMFI since early 2018, it seems appropriate for me to expound upon some of the special events that took place in the Fellowship's history. The organization had some special beginnings in 1951, 1952, and 1953, and thus it is common to hear or read of different years as to when FGBMFI was "founded," depending on the context and usage of the word. Surely, in many respects it "began" in 1951 with the first group meeting in Los Angeles. It was "established," or "founded," in 1952 with the signing of the Articles of Incorporation and acceptance of the organization's Constitution and Bylaws by the newly established officers, and at the end of 1952 Demos received an inspiring vision from God to continue the work. FGBMFI was officially "incorporated" in early 1953 with the state of California.

FGBMFI had its beginning in **1951**, the year when the first group meeting was held at Clifton's Cafeteria in Los Angeles, California. In the fall of 1951, Demos Shakarian shared his idea for the first time,[531] with Oral Roberts, of having a "Full Gospel" organization of businessmen where the men could share their experiences of God (e.g. testimonies) with other laymen.[532] Further, he shared the idea of naming the organization "Full Gospel Business Men's Fellowship International." Afterwards, with the help of Roberts as the first speaker, Demos started the first group meeting, at Clifton's Cafeteria in downtown Los Angeles on Saturday, October 13,

1951.[533] At the end of the meeting, Roberts prayed aloud unto God, "Let this Fellowship grow in Your strength alone...[to] a thousand chapters."[534] In preparation for the first official business meeting, organizational documents were drafted with the hired help of lawyer, Paul B. Fischer.[535] While the Los Angeles group met twice with small numbers (and eventually became the first official chapter), Demos held a group meeting at a restaurant in Fresno, California with 150 people on November 17, 1951. Immediately afterwards, they met and held the first official business meeting and agreed on a group name, which turned out to be temporary, and elected Demos Shakarian as its president.[536] According to Shakarian, FGBMFI started "Spiritually" at the first group meeting at Clifton's Cafeteria and started "Legally" a few weeks later at the business meeting in Fresno where the five-man board of directors signed the Articles of Incorporation,[537] albeit for the group name ending with "America" rather than "International." Thus, 1951 was a special beginning for FGBMFI,[538] as Demos Shakarian mentioned it "began" spiritually and legally in 1951[539] and mentions in retrospect that October 1952 was FGBMFI's first anniversary.[540]

FGBMFI was established, or founded, in **1952** when the five directors (including Demos Shakarian) adopted and signed the new Articles of Incorporation along with the Constitution and Bylaws (on November 22, 1952) for the newly named Full Gospel Business Men's Fellowship **International** (FGBMFI), which was followed by Demos receiving a vision from God encouraging him to continue the work globally. For many months prior to the signing, attorney Paul Fischer and Demos worked hard on a draft of the new Articles/Constitution/Bylaws, and when satisfied, they called for that special organizational meeting to approve the documents that would eventually be submitted to the state of California.[541] Demos Shakarian recalls those days in his article, "How Our Fellowship Came into Being," in the organization's first published *Voice* magazine in February 1953:

> Following this meeting [of over 100 Full Gospel Business Men in Phoenix, Arizona in January 1952], we engaged Paul B. Fischer, a Christian attorney who has had great experience in corporation organizational work, and he and I worked many days together. Finally, we

started reading our Documents to Pastors, Evangelists and Business Men. We kept working on our basic Documents until we felt we had the very finest Articles of Incorporation, By-laws, Constitution and Doctrinal Statement humanly possible to devise.

On November 22, 1952, came the signing of the Articles of Incorporation with a marvelous Ceremony at Clifton's Upper Room. All of the International Officers were present except Lee Braxton, who signed the Document later. The room was packed and the Spirit of God certainly stamped approval upon our efforts. As Earl Draper, Secretary-Treasurer, read the Doctrinal Statement, suddenly the Glory of God seemed to enter into the room, all started praising God, and Great rejoicing came forth. Following this, the Articles of Incorporation were signed, and G.H. Montgomery, Associate Editor of Healing Waters Magazine, Tulsa, Oklahoma, delivered a marvelous Dedicatory Message.[542]

Despite this jubilant occurrence, the Fellowship did not seem to be growing the way Demos expected.

While there was sporadic attendance at meetings throughout 1952, the same people kept coming without any new growth, and the attendance dropped in November and December, especially during the Christmas season. Despite how hard Demos tried to make it work, it was not growing and there was opposition from churches and no donations given. Observing the situation, Miner Arganbright, a director of the organization, reminded Demos that Demos had always called this Fellowship an "experiment," and Miner expressed his opinion that this experiment failed and that the organization was not worth even a nickel.[543] At the end of 1952, Demos became so discouraged to the point of shutting down the organization, but then he received a supernatural, life-transforming vision from God, on the evening of December 26, 1952, that re-ignited his dreams and encouraged him to move forward with the work of the Fellowship and to take the "global renewal" internationally. His wife, Rose, was in the room and encouraged Demos by interpreting this vision as saying that God wants the Fellowship "to go on" and not shut down.[544] Furthermore, on the next day, Shakarian was given additional support by Miner Arganbright, who then became the first during the entire year to donate to the organization (outside of Demos) with a significant amount of $1000, upon the leading of the Lord;[545] and further support was given that day by Thomas Nickel, who felt led to offer his printing press services for the Fellowship to have a voice, and encouraged the immediate publication of the first edition of *Voice* magazine, to be filled with inspirational content promoting testimonies and activities of FGBMFI. "The first official act of Full Gospel Business Men's Fellowship International was to select Thomas R. Nickel as Editor and Publisher, authorizing him to create and maintain an official publication, *Full Gospel Men's Voice*."[546] The magazine was edited by Nickel and first published two months later in February 1953.[547] For ten years, Thomas Nickel served as editor of *Voice* magazine. Demos appointed Jerry Jensen to follow after Nickel as editor in late 1962.[548] Even years later, Demos would look back and recall "with such joy" the day when both Arganbright and Nickel were used of the Lord to encourage him with the international vision.[549] Tallman writes, "For Shakarian, the organization was no longer his vision; it was God's vision...a divine mandate that could no longer be delayed."[550] Thus, the reception of the vision became the spiritual rebirth of the organization in 1952. Coupled with the Fellowship being legally grounded with signed documents reflecting the name *Full Gospel Business Men's Fellowship **International*** in 1952, profound action was taken by Demos and the directors, who were recharged after Demos received the vision to move the organization forward. The vision confirmed in his heart that the Fellowship needed to continue to exist and thrive. Before the vision, Demos speculated whether the experiment should continue; Now, Demos was moving forward with solidarity in heart, mind, soul, and body. Now, Demos knew in his innermost being that the Fellowship should continue, and thus the foundation had been laid. Consequentially, FGBMFI's official magazine, *Voice*, attributed a 1952 founding date.

Voice magazine stated in its editions, from 1984 to 1997, that FGBMFI was founded in **1952**. Starting in January 1984 with editor

Nelson B. Melvin, each edition of the *Voice* magazine included the following statement:

> "WHO WE ARE: Full Gospel Business Men's Fellowship International was **founded in 1952** by Demos Shakarian to reach men for Jesus. [Within that year], God gave him a vision of the people of every continent, revealing that the ministry of the Fellowship would result in people everywhere being brought to Jesus and linked in loving community. That vision is becoming a reality through the Fellowship's ministries..."[551]

When Jerry Jensen was once again editor of *Voice* in late 1985, this same verbiage was continued in each magazine up until April 1997,[552] and Jerry Jensen also included this same verbiage of "**founded in 1952**," in a special 40th Anniversary edition in late 1992 called *Vision: The Dawning of a New Day*.[553] Thus, it is very appropriate to say that FGBMFI was founded in 1952. Subsequently (or concurrently), Demos and the directors moved forward and submitted the signed Articles of Incorporation to the state of California, and FGBMFI was officially "incorporated" on January 2, 1953, as stated in every *Voice* magazine edition.[554]

The year **1953** started significantly for FGBMFI, as it was officially recognized as a religious non-profit organization on January 2, 1953, by the state of California under the name of *Full Gospel Business Men's Fellowship **International***, after which groups (i.e. chapters) were chartered under that name. This special date and a statement of incorporation were repeatedly specified in the editions of the Full Gospel Business Men's *VOICE* magazine.[555] Thus, some date the founding of the organization to 1953, the year FGBMFI was officially recognized and incorporated by the state of California as a religious non-profit organization.[556] Yet, the founding or birth of the organization really took place when Demos and the directors signed the new Articles of Incorporation, accepted the new Constitution and Bylaws, and were convinced of God's direction for the Fellowship as a result of the supernatural vision God gave to Demos and the dramatic confirmation from two key people under the leading of the Lord. This legal and spiritual rebirth provided the foundation. As an analogy, if a baby is born on a particular day and the paperwork eventually gets processed by the state a few days later, the birthdate is the day of birth regardless of when the state officially recognizes the birth. Since significant beginnings occurred in 1951, 1952, and 1953, it may be a matter of semantics as to whether FGBMFI was "founded" in 1951 or 1952 or 1953, based on spiritual and legal activity conducted in each of those years, along with an inner resolve to continue the organization. A generic statement could be used to encompass all three perspectives by saying FGBMFI was founded in the early 1950s, as there were significant events in the beginning of the Fellowship in 1951, 1952, and 1953. Nevertheless, it seems good to say that FGBMFI "began" in 1951, was established and "founded" in 1952, and "incorporated" in 1953. To celebrate these beginnings, the year 1953 was when the first National Convention was held in Los Angeles and attended by nine chapters and 600 people, from October 10-13, 1953, exactly two years after the first meeting in Clifton's Cafeteria.[557]

After a few years expanding within the United States, FGBMFI expanded internationally. With the chartering of a chapter in Johannesburg, South Africa in 1955,[558] and a Canadian chapter in Toronto in 1956, the organization became "international."[559] The October 1962 *Voice* magazine reported that Billy Graham spoke at FGBMFI's "10th Annual Convention" in Seattle on July 6, 1962.[560] The 14th Annual International Convention was held in Miami in 1967.[561] The 16th annual World convention in 1969 gathered 50,000 people in Washington, D.C.[562] The 18th World Convention was held in Denver in 1971.[563] By 1975, the Fellowship grew to have 1,650 chapters in fifty-two countries with average monthly attendance being over half a million,[564] which equates to about 300 attendees per chapter meeting. Thus, at this time, many were labeling the Fellowship as "the largest laymen's organization in the world."[565] One of FGBMFI's effective tools for reaching people with simple and dramatic testimonies was the "Good News" television show, which at its peak was broadcast to over 150 television stations and 70 radio stations.[566] In 1985, the 32nd World Convention of FGBMFI was held for the first time outside the USA in Melbourne, Australia, where evangelist Reinhard Bonnke was as a key speaker.[567] To help serve its worldwide vision and members, FGBMFI built a beautiful International Headquarters in Costa Mesa, California, encompassing 160,000 square feet with 125 employees.[568] The headquarters was dedicated in 1980. By 1988, FGBMFI had approximately 3,000 chapters in eighty-seven nations, with approximately two-thirds of the chapters (about 2,000 chapters) in the United States.[569] Further, international membership exceeded 33,000 and the Board of International Directors consisted of 140 members in 1988.[570] In the early years, the vast majority of International Directors were from the United States, yet by 1990, forty percent were from outside the United States. In the years 1990, 1991, 1992, and 1993, FGBMFI "was in" 106, 112, 115, and 120 countries, respectively.[571]

In July 1992, a year before the death of the founder and first International President, Demos Shakarian announced that his son Richard would eventually be his successor as the second International President.[572] Demos proceeded to sign an "Appointment of Successor" document in front of a Notary Public in the state of California on January 23, 1993, appointing Richard Shakarian as his initial successor, in accordance with the revised 1991 FGBMFI Bylaws. Demos died at the age of 80 on July 23, 1993, soon after the 40th World Convention in Boston, and his son assumed the role of International President. Despite some groups venturing apart to form new Full Gospel men's ministries, FGBMFI continued to expand.[573]

The Fellowship encountered several separate independent development initiatives (or splits). The first occurred in 1989 and was confined mostly to the United States, where roughly half of the worldwide membership existed. This resulted in the formation of the International Fellowship of Christian Businessmen (IFCB) in 1989. While IFCB did retain many of the main ideas and strategies of FGBMFI, they "did not include any references to Demos Shakarian, his vision, or his legacy in the formation of their organization."[574] In the years after the transition to a new International President in 1993, the Fellowship vision had experienced the birthing of three new development formations, working apart from the International Headquarters:

- In 1994-96, the formation of Business Men's Fellowship (including BMF USA, UK and Europe, BMF India, Brazil [later becoming ADHONEP] and independent FGBMF representations in Hong Kong, Malaysia, Singapore and some other nations).

- In 2006, the formation of FGBMF America and FGBMF Canada.
- In 2011, the independent development initiatives of the Fellowship in Nigeria, UK, Germany, Austria, Finland, and Russia.

At a Global Leadership Prayer Summit in 2012, the Full Gospel Global Forum (FGGF) was established, which eventually knit together many of those national organizations that were apart from the International Headquarters but were still following the Fellowship's God-given global vision, as shown to Demos Shakarian.[575] While many hearts have cried out for unity in working together, which can have a multiplied impact, sometimes working separately can be used of the Lord: Paul and Barnabas parted ways over their disagreement of whether to take Mark on their second journey, and yet both Paul and Barnabas were then used mightily of God in reaching the world for Christ in their separate ways; So too, God uses different ministries arising from different views and ways, to reach people for Jesus. Nevertheless, I pray as Jesus prayed (in John 17:20-23) for all believers to experience unity in fellowship and the Holy Spirit so that the world may know, in a greater way, the love of God and the truth that the Father has sent Jesus as Savior of the world. I rejoice that joint meetings in renewed fellowship and sharing have more recently taken place, since 2018, between FGBMFI and FGGF leaders in some major global regions.

After the passing away of Richard Shakarian in November 2017, the FGBMFI International Directors met in Houston, Texas, USA on February 10, 2018, and elected Mario Garcia Olvera (from Mexico) as the next International President of FGBMFI. Mario Garcia, a successful Christian businessman, previously served as FGBMFI Regional Vice President for Latin America and as President of FGBMFI Mexico. With an emphasis on diversity, under the leading of the Lord, International President Mario Garcia (from Mexico), appointed his cabinet: Francis Owusu (from Ghana) as International Treasurer, Douglas Woolley (from USA) as International Secretary, and Ardian Kristanto (from Indonesia) as International Executive Vice President. While touching over 85 nations, the FGBMFI global censuses of 2018, 2019, and 2020 reported that FGBMFI had active national organizations in more than 54 countries with over 4,300 chapters and more than 57,000 members. More than half of the membership of FGBMFI now resides in Latin America, who often reference the organization by its Spanish initials and name *FIHNEC (Fraternidad Internacional de Hombres de Negocios del Evangelio Completo)*.

Two top historians have provided their assessment of the impact of the Fellowship over the years upon society. Writing a year before the end of Demos' life, Vinson Synan boldly states, "The worldwide growth and influence of FGBMFI had succeeded in making this by far the most successful and far-reaching laymen's organization in the history of Christianity."[576] Two decades after Synan's bold assertion, Matthew Tallman brazenly writes, "over a half billion Christians today have been directly or indirectly influenced by Demos Shakarian and the organization he founded."[577]

Executive Ministries

Executive Ministries (now included in City Ministries in CRU) is an interdenominational ministry that has been helping to fulfill the Great Commission since the early 1960s by "reaching out to the executive, professional, and leadership community."[578] Their mission encompasses "turning influencers into Great Commission leaders." One of the ways of initially accomplishing this goal is through an Outreach Dinner Party, which "is an elegant social gathering in the non-threatening environment of a spacious home, country club or hotel."[579] A respectable speaker shares a concise message of their life after dinner to the 125 or more guests. The response at the conclusion of these dinner meetings is phenomenal, with over 30 percent of the guests indicating on comment cards "that they have prayed to receive Christ or would like to have more information about how to know Him personally."[580]

FCCI

Fellowship of Companies for Christ International (FCCI) is a non-denominational membership "organization that equips and encourages Christian business owners, executives, and professionals who desire to use their companies as platforms for ministry."[581] Their vision is to "transform the world through Christ, one company leader at a time."[582] Further, on their website, they state their mission as follows: "In pursuit of Christ's eternal objectives, we equip and encourage Christian business leaders to operate their businesses and conduct their personal lives in accordance with Biblical principles."[583] FCCI is using the brand name of Christ@Work within the USA.[584] Their strong points are "face to face training events" such as conferences and seminars. Starting in 1978, a small group of business owners met consistently for prayer and discussion of how to practically apply biblical principles to the operations of their businesses, after which FCCI was initially and formally incorporated in 1981, under the name of Fellowship of Companies for Christ (FCC).[585] In the mid-1980s, the vision had expanded to the global marketplace and thus the name became FCC International (FCCI). As of 2019, the president for FCCI is Lee Truax, who previously served as president of CBMC, Inc. from 2009 to 2017 and vice president for CBMC International from 2017 to 2019.

ICCC

International Christian Chamber of Commerce (ICCC) was founded in 1985 by Gunnar Olson, a Swedish industrialist. Before and after the founding of ICCC, Olson served as National President for FGBMFI Sweden for much of the 1980s. ICCC has expanded since 1985 to have members in 6 continents and representation in 75 nations, with ICCC leadership in 42 nations, as of 2020.[586] ICCC's mission is "to serve as a vehicle in extending the operation and principles of wisdom, love and rule of God into the marketplace of the world."[587] Further ICCC's vision is stated as "A **worldwide people** who, in their **business** and **working lives**, are **experiencing the reality** of goals, strategies, and plans, becoming an outward **manifestation**

of an inward walk of **faith**, leading to a **glorious release** of the **Kingdom of God**."[588] Further, ICCC states that its purpose is "to encourage and equip Christians ... to experience a release into a new dimension of Faith, Hope, Love. and Freedom in their business and working lives."[589] ICCC is a non-denominational organization that has a long and close relationship with FGBMFI, though their focus is slightly different. The website for ICCC describes their organizational distinction as follows:

> *ICCC is an official Chamber of Commerce with a mandate to connect businesses and promote business activity among its members, while it also exists to provide practical, biblical teaching and training for those engaged in the Marketplace. ICCC has a number of International projects underway at any given time and is regularly called upon to assist national governments on specific initiatives relating to commerce.*[590]

Gunnar Olson of ICCC has been instrumental in encouraging Os Hillman, who started another Faith at Work organization. It is interesting to note that CBMC influenced Demos Shakarian as its chapter president, who went on to found FGBMFI, which influenced Gunnar Olson as National President of FGBMFI Sweden, who founded ICCC, which influenced Os Hillman, who founded Market Place Leaders. Likewise, one of the founding members and area coordinators of FCCI was Buck Jacobs,[591] who subsequently founded another organization, the C12 Group, dedicated to helping Christians at work.

C12 Group

The **C12 Group**, founded in 1992 by Buck Jacobs in Tampa, Florida, is a prominent Christian leadership development organization. The "C" in the "C12" name represents "Christian," and the "12" represents the group of twelve disciples of Jesus, and 12 is believed to be an efficient number of members for a small group. C12 is the USA's largest network of Christian CEOs, business owners, and executives, who share ideas monthly with like-minded peers in groups and encourage one another to honor God in their business conduct.[592] Their mission is to "equip Christian CEOs and owners to build great businesses for a greater purpose" and their vision is "to change the world by advancing the Gospel in the marketplace."[593] They emphasize "incorporating business best practices with the foundation of Biblical principles and core values" as well as being "Ambassadors for Christ in the marketplace."[594] Many employees, customers, and suppliers have come to the Lord as a result of being touched by the example and witness of a C12 member company.[595] While many C12 local groups exist throughout the USA, there is also an international presence in Brazil, Malaysia, and Singapore.[596] The current President and CEO for C12 Group is Mike Sharrow.

CMDL

The **Coalition for Ministry in Daily Life (CMDL)** was founded in 1991 by Bill Diehl (a Lutheran), who transitioned leadership in the late 1990s to Sally Simmel, Pete Hammond, and others.[597] "CMDL provided a venue for Mainline Protestants, Evangelicals and Roman Catholics to connect and collaborate."[598] "The Coalition for Ministry in Daily Life is an international network of Christians and their organizations committed to fostering the affirmation and practice of ministry in daily life by all followers of Christ."[599] The coalition endeavors to:

[1] Support one another's efforts to continue Christ's ministry in daily life and become part of the Spirit's movement in our time;

[2] Provide opportunities for Christians from different traditions, places and occupations to learn from each other about their ministries in the workplace, the community and the family;

[3] Commend to all our sisters and brothers in Christ the theological perspectives, institutional patterns and personal practices that are especially supportive of ministry in daily life.[600]

While CMDL connected mostly with Protestants and some Catholics and Evangelicals until the organization ended in 2011, Os Hillman was able to form two organizations that connected especially with

"Independents and Charismatics," though not limited to these groups, as he sponsored "annual national gatherings."[601]

Marketplace Leaders

Marketplace Leaders, whose founder and president is Os Hillman, seeks to train people to see their work as a calling and a ministry. Their vision is to "transform leaders to transform culture," by restoring biblical foundations in our nation's seven cultural mountains.[602] They have worked towards this since their founding in 1996 and continue to do so by building unity among marketplace ministries, publishing resources for workplace Christians, providing consultation for companies desiring to implement biblical principles, and training new leaders through a one-day workshop, *The 9 to 5 Window Workshop* (previously named *Called to the Workplace—From Esau to Joseph*).[603] One of their main tools is a free devotional for people in the workplace, *TGIF Today God is First*, which has been very popular among a quarter of a million recipients. One of the ways the organization builds unity among marketplace ministries is through Hillman's other ministry, **International Coalition of Workplace Ministries (ICWM)**, a division of Marketplace Leaders Ministries. ICWM functions as a coalition, a fellowship, or an alliance of believers who are leaders of organizations or workplace ministries and "who want to encourage and unite leaders by inspiring, connecting, and equipping them for transformation of the workplace for Christ."[604] ICWM helps by providing "resources, information and networking to organizations that are also called to this mission" of transformation.[605]

Analysis of Groups

Many of these earlier groups such as CBMC, FGBMFI, Executive Ministries, FCCI, and the C12 Group, have focused on a particular segment of society, such as businesspersons or executives. While these groups still have a desirable focus, many other groups and people aspire to reach out more broadly to all workers, including stay-at-home moms, students, vocational ministers, and the typical employee who reports to a boss. Hillman states:

One of the key differences in the modern-day movement is that the focus is no longer evangelism to male executives. The modern-day movement is focused on a more holistic approach to apply faith in the realm where so many people spend so much of their time—their work life. These include students, housewives, those in the military, executives, nurses, doctors, lawyers, and people in entertainment and government. Ministries are no longer just birthing outside the local church as para-church ministries, but local churches are now recognizing the need to equip their people and release them into their workplaces as extended missions of their churches.[606]

For groups with a broader and more holistic approach, "Evangelism is not an end goal of workplace ministry; it is the fruit. It is about experiencing the fullness of God in all aspects of [their] work life."[607]

"We're all called to the mission field. It is a matter of which mission field."

Os Hillman

CHAPTER THIRTEEN
SOME PRACTICAL IMPLICATIONS

Implications from Teachings in Some Faith at Work Organizations

Each one of the Faith at Work organizations profiled in the previous section are major players in assisting Christians in integrating their faith with their work. Perhaps one of these excellent organizations can guide you further in your desire to implement the practical implications of a theology of work. Many of these organizations train Christians, and provide opportunities for them, to reach out to non-Christians in hopes of drawing them closer to a personal relationship with Jesus Christ. Such an emphasis is surely the heartbeat of God. Some of these organizations emphasize other aspects of faith that people can implement in their work setting. While people can draw many implications from the various teachings in the assortment of Faith at Work organizations, I have homed in on discussing just a few implications from two organizations.

Os Hillman, president of Marketplace Leaders, emphasizes in *Faith & Work* that there is no distinction in the eyes of God between sacred and secular work; all workers are called to "have an overriding ministry objective to reflect Christ's love and power in [their] lives."[608] Thus, Hillman is in favor of replacing misunderstood terminology, which may carry a connotation of spiritual superiority that makes others feel like second-class citizens in the kingdom of God, with biblical terminology. For example, it is common to hear that "only missionaries and preachers are in full time Christian work," but Hillman insists, "we're all in full time Christian work, however, some are called to vocational ministry."[609] Some may say "I'm called to the mission field," but Hillman says, "We're all called to the mission field. It is a matter of which mission field. There is no greater mission field than the marketplace...God wants to reach these people just as much as those who have not heard in foreign lands."[610] Some may say "I'm in the ministry," but all Christians are in the ministry as they walk out their faith.[611] All Christians have as much a ministry as a pastor or priest, just a different mission field. Thus, Hillman prefers the phrase "vocational ministry" instead of "ministry" or "full-time ministry" or "full-time Christian work."[612] In summary, "we need both a terminology and a mind-set that works to eliminate the 'second-class citizen' concept in the Kingdom of God."[613]

One practical way to be prepared for ministry at the workplace is to put God and His Kingdom first in one's thoughts and actions, thereby affecting the rest of the day. One of the means to accomplish this is to dedicate a little time each morning to prayer and a biblical devotion. Os Hillman is famous for producing excellent daily devotionals on the Internet. Many of them are compiled into his book *TGIF: Today God is First* containing marketplace meditations grouped by themes such as adversity, calling, and decision-making. The largest number of meditations falls in the section "calling," which is reflective of Hillman's emphasis that work for a Christian is a calling to ministry.[614] Some other devotionals that help one to focus on God and His relevant role at one's work include Wally Kroeker's *God's Week has 7 Days* that highlights some areas where faith and ethics intersect with real work;[615] Andria Hall's *The Walk at Work* that helps one find "soul satisfaction" in the workplace;[616] Barbara Smith-Moran's *Soul at Work* that reflects on spirituality of everyday work;[617] and Edward Grube's *Coffee Break Meditations* containing 260 meditations for the workplace.[618] The following books are also devotional tools to focus on God and are geared toward leading an individual or group into a Bible Study of work related topics: Marilyn Kunz and Catherine

Schell's *Work—God's Gift*;[619] Robert Banks and Gordon Preece's *Getting the Job Done Right*;[620] R. Paul Stevens and Gerry Schoberg's *Satisfying Work*;[621] Thomas Nelson Publishers' *Making Your Work Count for God*,[622] and more recently the Theology of Work Project's multi-volume *The Bible and Your Work Study Series*.[623]

Many of the workplace ministries and leaders strongly associated with Os Hillman have been emphasizing societal transformation. Peter Wagner, for example, says that he and other apostolic leaders are hearing a specific word or direction from the Spirit, namely "social transformation!"[624] Wagner further says that the church "is to aggressively seek to take dominion of the society in which we live."[625] In "Session 5" of Hillman's workshop, Hillman emphasizes that God wants transformation in the workplace and not just evangelization, since God is interested in the Kingdom and not just adding to the church:

> *Many times the local church focuses only on the Gospel of Salvation instead of the Gospel of the Kingdom, and Jesus spoke more about the Kingdom than he did of the Gospel of Salvation...If* [God] *only wanted salvation, we'd all die and go to heaven right after we got saved, but He really wants to have His Kingdom on earth as it is in heaven as he prayed in the Lord's Prayer. And so He leaves us here in order to usher in that* [transformation] *in the world we live in.*[626]

Hillman adds in *The 9 to 5 Window*, "While salvation is part of bringing the kingdom of God on Earth, it includes much more."[627] Some of their teaching on social transformation and its implications come close to the controversial tenets of "Dominion Theology" or "Kingdom Now Theology," such as "the belief that the church is to exercise rule over every area of society, people as well as institutions, before Christ returns" and that "this current age is the kingdom of God spoken of in the Bible,...[and therefore] Christians are currently responsible, by God's power, to see that it is developed to maturity."[628] To hold these beliefs, one must espouse some kind of postmillennialism.[629] By emphasizing and proclaiming distinctive postmillennial beliefs, within a Faith at Work context, workplace leaders risk alienating a large portion of diverse workplace Christians who hold to premillennialism or amillennialism.

For years, Thomas Ice tried to blend a Reconstructionist view of social transformation with premillennialism but concluded that the two are incompatible.[630] The former view teaches that people can establish the kingdom of God during this era prior to Christ's return whereas premillennialism teaches that Christ will come and destroy the established society in judgment prior to His millennial reign.[631] In addition, "dominionists do not believe in a literal catching up of the Church to be with the Lord"; instead, they believe that Jesus will return at the completion of the millennium or after the Church begins ruling society.[632] According to Albert Dager, "Many premillennialists are beginning to buy into the dominion concept," though not completely, and thus "call themselves 'premillennial dominionists', who believe that the rapture will occur after the Church has taken dominion to some extent, but before the millennial reign of Jesus is established."[633] Premillennialists hold the "biblical truth that when Jesus returns the nations will be allied against Him, not waiting to welcome Him with open arms (**Matthew 24; Mark 13; Revelation 6-7**; [**Revelation 16:14, 19:19**])."[634] Wagner, who acknowledges teaching a Dominion Theology, says, "For most of the twentieth century, the prevailing eschatology (doctrine of the end times) of evangelicals was premillennialism."[635] Thus, some in the body of Christ are apt to reject current aspects of teaching in segments of the Faith at Work movement that emphasizes Dominion Theology and Kingdom Now Theology unless they have a "paradigm shift toward social transformation" and its logical conclusion.[636]

Another emphasis, among some leaders and workplace ministries strongly associated with Os Hillman, has been the need to restore the offices of apostles and prophets and to recognize them within the workplace. This view is especially held by those who are members of the International Coalition of Apostles (ICA), whose Presiding Apostle has been Dr. Peter Wagner since its inception in 1999. Since many denominations, such as the Assemblies of God, do not recognize the titles or offices of apostles and prophets today,[637] some Christian leaders and participants in legitimate Faith at Work organizations may feel uncomfortable with such controversial teaching. However, for many others, such views may be propelling them to action.

Kent Humphreys, who served as president of FCCI starting in 2002, provides a practical strategy and guide for pastors to equip workplace leaders to influence their workplaces in his book *Lasting Investments*. Humphreys encourages pastors to develop relationships with church members and meet with a small group of six to twelve workplace leaders—"people with a good heart and those that have influence at work and in the community... who are 'change agents' not really satisfied with the status quo."[638] Humphreys states, "The goal of such a small-group meeting would be to help these leaders figure out how to have an effective ministry in their own spheres of influence."[639] As a further emphasis, Humphreys says, "Remember, you are not recruiting this group of leaders to the church's activities or to your ministry, but you are asking them to allow you to help them be used by God where they are."[640] A pastor should ask the question, "How may I help you [to minister in the workplace where God has placed you]?"[641] As the group continues to meet, it is good for the pastor to slip back a bit and allow them to strategize with each other on how they could influence their particular workplaces for Christ. According to Humphreys, these leaders desire to make a lasting investment which can only happen by impacting the lives of people for eternity, using their workplace as a platform for ministry, which "must have as its long-term eternal focus either evangelism or discipleship as defined by Jesus in the Great Commission (see **Matthew 28:19-20**)."[642] Thus, ministry does not include the meeting of temporal needs, such as feeding the hungry, unless its focus is on the eternal, according to Humphreys.[643]

Practical Thoughts about Career Decision and Work Connected to God

When needing to determine a career or a job to pursue, one must discern whether God is leading or calling them to a particular field along with one's gifts and talents and desires. R. J. Rushdoony sees career counseling as disastrous when it advises a student to go into a work area that may be more profitable but not the area for which he has a calling, an interest, or a talent. Due to a surplus of engineers in the early 1970s, Rushdoony saw many students of engineering steered "into businesses or types of work they were not geared to," which produced many unhappy young people.[644] Instead of looking at employment "purely in terms of economics," Rushdoony says people should pursue their calling, for "a person can be very much underpaid and be happy if their work is their calling."[645] Bernbaum and Steer say that overemphasizing the scriptural evidence that God calls people into Christian-service careers causes people to "mystify the call to Christian service" and "assign all other careers to a non-call, non-spiritual status," yet God can guide people into other careers and both require prayer, self-examination, a thorough study of alternatives, and a careful and honest assessment of God-given abilities and talents.[646] Higginson says that a sense of vocation must be accompanied by evidence of having the necessary attributes, such as a clergyperson having pastoral sensitivity or an artisan having manual dexterity. If there is no evidence, then the person must reassess their understanding of God's vocational call on their life, for "ideally vocation and gift should be complementary concepts."[647] Andy Mills goes a step further to say, "If we are not walking in our gifting, then we are outside the will of God for our lives."[648] Being good stewards of what God has given a person is a topic woven throughout the Scriptures[649] and this includes being a good steward of their gifts and talents as well. Thus, if a person's strengths are not fitting their job (and if it is possible to have other options and there is a desire to do so), then they can be a better steward of the gifts by looking out for a job or assignment that would better use their unique gifts,[650] which would manifest in greater satisfaction and greater returns on the investment, both for self and those served. Nevertheless, if the ideal job is not available, a person may need to swallow one's pride and vanity of expecting a grandiose job and be grateful to have some kind of work that simply pays the bills to support one's self and family, and such work is a gift from God.[651] If a person hates their job, God's guidance can bring them to different job, or God's guidance can help them do their job more meaningfully.[652]

SOME PRACTICAL IMPLICATIONS

Christians desperately need to know that their work matters to God and that it is actually connected to what God wants done in this world. As a model, Jesus always did what He saw the Father doing (**John 5:19**). Gordon Preece aptly says, "By seeing our work in the light of God's work, we can see God's hand in our everyday tasks."[653] Those who minister in a church or to the spiritual needs of individuals have an easier time seeing the connection between this work and God's work. Sherman and Hendricks have found that workers in secular occupations and especially those "who deal with data and things as opposed to people" are more likely to feel that their work does not contribute to God's work.[654] Those in caring professions such as psychologists, social workers, doctors, and nurses have an easier time seeing their work as related to God's work.[655] Alistair Mackenzie came to similar conclusions after conducting six months of in-depth interviews with over one hundred Christians about their faith and work. Mackenzie found:

> *There were certain categories of people who really struggled to see that their work mattered from God's perspective at all...*[yet] *people who are involved in more direct, person-to-person, service kind of jobs feel that their work counts from God's perspective. Social workers, doctors, nurses, teachers,* [and to some extent parents who are working at home devoting time to their families]—*somehow the church affirms that their work is ministry...*[Others struggle to make a connection including] *factory workers, manufacturers, many business people and those involved in commercial or industrial work— those who feel somewhat removed from meeting people at their particular point of need.... A similar struggle is experienced by people who are involved in primarily technical jobs, where they are* [utilizing] *practical skills rather than being in direct contact with other people.*[656]

From these results, people seem to feel disconnected from God when they cannot see that their particular work really serves people or serves people in a way that God wants them served. Yet practically all jobs have a part in serving people when seen from a broader perspective, and God wants to meet all kinds of human needs out of love for people. Though not exhaustive, the Bible shows God as working in many different capacities to meet human needs: Some biblical metaphors describe God as a worker, builder, potter, shepherd, etc., which offer "a point of real connection with God and therefore a source of meaning and spirituality."[657] People should be able to see God's ongoing work on earth in each person's work, giving value to that work in God's sight.

CONCLUSION

In conclusion, work is a gift from God, but sin has affected work in the Fall and become more difficult and less enjoyable than it was originally. Reality is that a majority of people are unhappy with many aspects of their work—even Christians and some in vocational ministry. People often regard work as a curse and feel it is "a necessary evil," as many have thought in the past. Work can be a drag or a drudge, having to constantly wake up to an alarm clock, possibly putting in overtime or working the weekends, having difficulties with the bosses or coworkers or customers, making mistakes, commuting, getting called-out in the middle of the night, or trying to meet deadlines.[658] An adverse work environment can drag down, at times, even people who get to work a job for which that they are passionate. Work's pressure and stress frustrate people frequently, and they often encounter strife, resentment, fatigue, and apathy in their jobs; further, many are dissatisfied with their work, which they feel is unfulfilling, lacks meaning, without purpose, often not challenging, often repetitive, and often depersonalized.[659] The book of **Ecclesiastes** acknowledges that life and work in a fallen world is meaningless, apart from God. We need to update our thinking with the Word of God (**Rom. 12:1**) to see what God says about the value of work and how we ought to regard it, which will begin to improve our attitudes and feelings about work, which will help improve our behavior and performance at work.

It is encouraging seeing the growth of the number of published books and journal articles on "Theology of Work." The monumental work of the recently published *Theology of Work Bible Commentary* will be helpful to scholars, pastors, and workplace practitioners for years to come. Yet, different scholars in this field rightly express a need for more academic writings on this subject. In my book, from the discussion dealing with various aspects of a theology of work, people can recognize the practical implications that work is meaningful, purposeful, significant, and valuable, in the eyes of God. Work becomes most significant when it goes beyond just working for one's own needs or for society's needs, to working for God and with God to meet the needs of society and one's self. When connected with God, work is significant, for God is a worker and imparts purpose and meaning into work.

Recognizing and appreciating implications of a theology of work is crucial for workers—accountants to zoologists—to see their work as "more than a job."[660] For the Bible's teaching on work to be relevant to all people, writers must broaden the cultural definition of work as "paid employment" to include home duties, voluntary workers, and unemployed people who are utilizing their gifts in service to others. By seeing work as cooperating with God in His work of serving the needs of people, both spiritual and physical needs, all Christians can participate in work in this manner. Instead of making people into gods or reducing them to the level of animals, work makes people "into God's representatives on earth, his stewards, entrusted with the task of developing the rich resources of the earth for the benefit of the human community."[661] Furthermore, all people are expected to work, and the Bible gives no indication that work is to be avoided in life; instead, work is given as a divine command to Adam, a regulation in the Mosaic Law, an admonition in the Wisdom literature and in Paul's letters, and an example of Jesus' early life as a carpenter.[662] All who work can and should see their work as having a divine purpose, meaning, significance, and value.

History of Attitudes about Work

Over the years, people have held various views toward work. The Greeks and the Romans primarily saw manual labor as a curse and degrading for humans. The Jews and first century Christians elevated work as they served a God who works and who desires all people to work too. Over the next 1400 years, the Christian church gradually made a distinction between secular work and sacred work and elevated the latter as being more spiritual and pleasing to God. The Reformation captured an important truth that all human work, as long as it serves a person's neighbors, is pleasing to God. The Puritans emphasized diligent work unto Christ, but the concept of working unto God was lost during the Enlightenment Period and Industrial Revolution, thereby secularizing the Protestant work ethic. From the Industrial Revolution came a gradual exodus of women into the workforce to find meaningful work that society had taken out of their home. During the past two centuries, churches have struggled to find balance between working for transformation of society in accordance with the Cultural Mandate (**Gen. 1-2**) and working for evangelistic purposes in accordance with the Great Commission (**Matt. 28:19-20**).

Individuals in society today also have various views toward work, some of which stem from previous eras. Workaholics are a phenomenon of modern society, yet many in society also hate their jobs and prefer to get by doing as little work as possible in order to maximize their leisure time. Both overworking and under-working are displeasing to God. Some people view work, with its stress and monotony, as a curse resulting from the Fall. In today's industrial and informational society, people talk more about survival in one's job than about fulfillment in one's job. Sometimes people think the holy people for the Lord do "spiritual work", while "secular work" is done by those who don't measure up and have to settle for making money to pay bills for essentials. Many Christians who desire to please God feel that their secular work is not as pleasing to God as full-time vocational ministry work and that their work is not as beneficial to God's Kingdom. Christians must discover a proper theology of work because many of them feel their ordinary work does not really matter to God—sometimes due to an overemphasis on the importance of evangelism and work associated with the church.

THE VALUE OF WORK IN THE EYES OF GOD

Principles of a Biblical Theology of Work

Work is valuable to God because it is His nature to work. God created the universe and keeps it going through work. Because God works and calls His work "good," work is intrinsically good. He also created humankind in His image and thus they also have a nature to work; therefore, their work has dignity. God then gave man a command to work purposefully for Him and with Him in cooperation—the Creation Mandate. Work in cooperation with God is very meaningful. Contrary to the thoughts of some, the biblical evidence points to the fact that humankind worked prior to the Fall, and thus work is not a curse upon mankind, but instead work is a gift from God that carries purpose. In God's providence of sustaining creation, all legal and moral jobs, careers, and tasks have significance and value to God. God gives all people the opportunity to be co-workers with God, to bring about His purposes on earth, which includes personal redemption and societal transformation.

According to some theologians, such redemptive and transformational work done in accordance with God's purposes, God will preserve in the world to come. Yet, if God destroys the old earth and the new earth is created "from nothing," as in the annihilationist view, then the notion of work having a contribution in the new creation becomes invalid. However, if Goosen, Volf, and Cosden are correct in saying that the new creation will be a transformation of the old creation and that God will raise human work and purify it to shape eternity, then each person's work has eternal value and meaning in God's sight and in the new earth. Regardless, God will certainly preserve each person's work in His memory and reward the works with an inheritance by the Lord (**Col. 3:23-24**). There is significance and meaning in human work because God instituted work, made man to work, commands man to work, enables man to work alongside Him for His purposes, and establishes and rewards work.

Work can be satisfying, for it is a virtue originating in creation, but "it can also be frustrating, pointless, and exhausting" because work has been "tainted by sin" from the Fall.[663] Placher says work can be both a blessing that gives fulfillment and meaning in life and a curse that is burdensome and something to "endure" to pay for food and other necessities.[664] A proper view of work embraces both perspectives—its affirmation and its reality.

The Bible provides several purposes for working. Through work, people can glorify God as they work unto Christ, their ultimate boss (**Col. 3:23-24**). Thus, Christians should work with a different motive than non-Christians. Work enables one to meet personal and family needs. Work also enables one to help others in need. In God's providence, one's work enables others in society to have their needs met. Work can also assist the Great Commission as one earns and gives finances to people who spread the gospel; a good worker can also be a witness in deed and word, especially as one builds relationships that become opportunities for verbal witness. Another biblical purpose for working is for personal fulfillment.

All legal and moral jobs, careers, and tasks have significance and value to God. Since there "truly is no division between sacred and secular," Dallas Willard says "holy people must stop going into 'church work' as their natural course of action and take up holy orders in farming, industry, law, education, banking, and journalism with the same zeal previously given to evangelism or to pastoral and missionary work."[665] While a few ought to leave their secular employment for vocational ministry, most should remain where they are and "make their Christian witness *in* ordinary work rather than beyond it," as Elton Trueblood says.[666] In remaining in one's secular employment, a believer can allow Christ to transform oneself, thereby transforming the workplace.

God calls people to believe in Christ and follow Him, and while some may express that call by eventually leaving their everyday work-life to minister to the spiritual needs of people on a full-time basis, there is no call in the New Testament for all Christians to abandon their daily work. All kinds of work performed by a Christian is to be done unto Christ and for His glory (**Col. 3:23-24**) and will be rewarded accordingly. Having a full-time job does not make one a part-time Christian. All Christians are to be full-time Christians. Paul was a great model in that he worked as a tentmaker and often self-financed his ministry work. However, work does not just enable one to minister outside of work hours, but one's work—performed unto the Lord and to serve people—is a ministry in itself even if religious discussion does not take place.

When a connection can be made between God's work and one's job, a person does not need to quit their job upon becoming a Christian or upon realizing one needs to work for the Lord, for a person's job is already pleasing to the Lord as it serves other people and is done unto Christ. While some may sense God's calling to minister to the spiritual needs of people, others may remain in the calling of the job God has currently given them.

Christians should recognize that all lawful work (for a Christian) is a service of God, thus Christians should be the last people to look down on someone because of their job since God gave them that job. According to Rayburn, "the Lord is far more pleased with a devout [manual] laborer who serves Him in his daily work than a proud professor or entrepreneur who does not."[667]

God gives gifts and abilities to people to work in serving the needs of society. Often one's vocation or calling will involve utilizing these gifts and talents. Admittedly, a person who utilizes many of their unique gifts and talents will have a greater chance of being passionate about their job, which is a contributing factor in giving the worker a sense of fulfillment. However, sometimes, due to circumstances beyond one's control, a person may be underemployed with labor that is beneath his or her mental or physical abilities. According to the Reformers, in God's providence, even this work is a calling from God, and one should derive meaning and satisfaction in knowing that they have a ministry unto God and unto people. A person's attitude and behaviors can transform work that initially seems boring, frustrating, or meaningless.

While the Bible does not say as much about the kind of work one should pursue, it does say much about the way in which a worker should do his or her work. The Bible disapproves of laziness and idleness but highly regards the diligent worker who performs work with excellence. A Christian should be characterized by contentment and joy in working, as work is a gift from God. The Bible says that employees are to be respectful and faithful to their bosses, and likewise bosses are to be fair and just to their employees.

With such a high view of work in the Scriptures, one could mistakenly idolize work and become a workaholic to the neglect of other significant priorities, yet God wants to have people balancing their work with rest, with worship of Him, and with time spent with family and friends. Thus, God commanded a Sabbath rest in the days of Moses to regulate excessive work, and the spirit of such a command is very appropriate for working society today, as well. Some leisure activities can be a means of rejuvenating one's mind and body, yet other leisure activities do not provide such rest. While retirement may be a time for more rest due to one's old age, it is really a time to redirect one's means of serving other people and God.

As the subject of "theology of work" matures, more scholars will be discovering, developing, and expounding on different models for understanding work as given in the Bible. While the number of published books on the subject of "theology of work" and "faith at work" has grown considerably over the past few decades, experts have said there still needs to be more scholarly works produced in this area. One such book is by David Miller, who developed an "Integration Box" model to express ways that individuals and groups seek to integrate faith and work, via ethics, evangelism, experience, and enrichment. Miller has also served as an expert on the Faith at Work movement.

Faith at Work Movement

The Faith at Work movement is predominantly Christian-based and "organized around a quest to integrate one's personal faith teachings with one's professional work responsibilities."[668] While a few authors have grouped some non-Christian religious/spiritual workplace groups under the name "Faith at Work," the common understanding among the vast majority is that the Faith at Work movement is exclusively Christian while the "Workplace Spirituality" movement encompasses all spiritual groups. The Faith at Work movement is a broad term designated to describe the many diverse Christian ministries, conferences, e-newsletters, websites, books, magazines, podcasts, and radio shows that assist all people groups throughout the world in integrating faith with their "work." More recently, some within the movement have expanded the definition of "work" to include all who work, and not just those who are paid for their work.

Among the many organizations that serve people in integrating faith and work are CBMC, FGBMFI, Executive Ministries, FCCI, ICCC, C12 Group, CMDL, and Marketplace Leaders. The ministries of CBMC and FGBMFI pioneered the efforts of the Faith at Work movement in the 1930s and 1950s, respectively. In general, the earlier ministries focus on evangelism while the latter ministries incorporate a more holistic approach. CBMC, FGBMFI, Executive Ministries, and FCCI have all been effective in casting a vision for members to see their workplace as a potential platform for evangelism where members can build relationships and invite acquaintances to join other professional workers at outreach meetings or conferences sponsored by the respective ministries. Many of the latter ministries emphasize that Christians should work with excellence and proper ethics, with evangelism being a fruit (instead of an end goal) of incorporating faith with work.

There should be a balance between the Creation Mandate and the Great Commission, whereas in the past few decades, for the most part, mainline denominations and European churches have emphasized the Creation Mandate while evangelical churches have emphasized evangelism.[669] When unbalanced, those who only focus on the Creation Mandate are reluctant to engage in evangelism or cross-cultural missionary service, and those who only focus on the Great Commission are reluctant to care for the earth's resources or to place any intrinsic value in secular work itself. Church leadership is vital, and the Great Commission is essential, but people should also balance the Creation Mandate in importance.

Although a goal of social transformation may motivate believers to work hard unto the Lord in preparation for His return, many Christian denominations do not see social transformation as the ultimate goal or a realistic goal nor do they believe that humanity can usher in the kingdom of God prior to the dramatic return of Christ. Thus, such messages coming from a workplace ministry could cause pastors, whose end-time views differ, to feel uncomfortable about having their church members participate in that group. Of course, the reverse effect could result as well, and pastors who agree with such end-time views may encourage their members to participate even more. Furthermore, many church groups that are premillennial are recognizing the need to be involved in social transformation.

Christians desiring to serve God in the workplace can derive several practical implications. For example, desiring to put God first in one's life and to prepare oneself for the workday, Christians can start their day reading a daily devotional geared toward workers and real-life situations at work. Additionally, Christians can be more conscious of terminology that they use that may make people employed in secular jobs feel like second-class citizens in the kingdom of God when, in actuality, they too are in full-time Christian work, in full-time ministry, and called to a particular mission field. People often understand "ministry" as "the act of serving" in evangelism, worship, or edification of believers; however, with God's empowerment, coupled with proper understanding and attitudes about work, Christians can turn their jobs into ministry by living out their faith at work. God does call some people specifically to "vocational ministry" to lead the church and equip its members in works of service. Pastors have a great opportunity of helping their working members, especially those who are "workplace leaders," by arranging small group meetings and inspiring them to brainstorm some practical ways of living out their faith at work and becoming influencers at work.

Closing Comments

As Christians begin to see their work as participation with God's ongoing work of creating, sustaining, redeeming, and transforming, then they will see their work as having meaning and spiritual value both to them and to God. Also, as Christians work whole-heartedly unto Christ their boss—offering one's body in service to God—work then becomes a means of worship to God. Furthermore, such workers who are passionate about their work will inevitably be better workers, as they endeavor to serve other people as well as God.

Christians desperately need to know that their work has value in the eyes of God and that it connects to what God wants done in this world. As a model example, Jesus always did what He saw the

Father doing (**John 5:19**). Preece aptly says, "By seeing our work in the light of God's work, we can see God's hand in our everyday tasks."[670] God's work is a model for people; and one's work should connect with God's work. Christians will have a sense of purpose and fulfillment in their work, in part, to the degree in which they see their work as a reflection of God's work on the earth. The work of pastors, evangelists, and apologists seems to connect readily to God's own work as Redeemer. Yet, "the work God does is far broader than Christ's work of reconciling people or helping them grow together in faith and obedience."[671] While redemption is central in God's plan for man, "God is also Creator, Sustainer, Preserver, Provider, Revealer, and Lawgiver."[672] Therefore, when people perform some work that emulates God's work, they feel a connection, as a doctor may reflect God's desire and work to heal people. In essence, whenever anyone is serving the real needs of people, spiritual or physical, he or she is reflecting God's work of providentially meeting the needs of society; thus, work becomes meaningful, purposeful, significant, and valuable. A person should then be able to say, "My work is God's work."[673]

TABLES

Table 1

Impact of long hours[674]

	1997	1999
	%	%
No time for other interests:	77	87
Damaging health:	59	71
Affects relationship negatively with children:	73	86
with partner:	72	79
Reduces productivity over time:	55	68

Source: *The Quality of Working Life, 1999, Survey of Managers' Changing Experiences, Les Worrall & Cary Cooper, Institute of Management.*

GLOSSARY

amillennialism: the belief that the millennium in the Book of Revelation is symbolic of "fullness" or "completeness" and not literally a one-thousand-year period.

annihilationist: a belief that God will destroy the current earth by His judgment in preparation for the creation of a new heaven and a new earth "out of nothing."

calling: "to urgently invite someone to accept responsibilities for a particular task, implying a new relationship to the one who does the calling."[675]

co-creationism: view that creation was not entirely finished in **Genesis 1-2**, and humans participate and contribute toward God's continuous activity of creation.

Creation Mandate: mandate from God to rule over, care for, and serve the rest of God's creation (**Gen. 1:26-30; 2:15**). Sometimes it is called the Cultural Mandate.

Cultural Mandate: mandate from God to transform society (**Gen. 1-2**).

Dominion Theology: belief that the Church will take dominion over all of society prior to Jesus' return.

dominionist: one who ascribes to Dominion Theology.

eschatological: having to do with the last events of time, such as the new heaven and new earth.

eschatology: a branch of theology dealing with final events of time, such as the return of Christ.

exegetes: people who interpret and explain the Bible text.

Evangelistic Mandate: mandate from God to save souls (**Matt. 28:19-20**).

Faith at Work movement: a movement of individuals and groups interested in integrating personal faith with one's work.

full-time Christian ministry (common definition): going overseas as a missionary, becoming a minister in the church, or doing something for a Christian organization.

Great Commission: to go and make disciples of Jesus Christ and teach them (**Matt. 28:19-20**).

kingdom of God: renewal of all creation by the re-entry of God's ruling power through Christ's death and resurrection.

Kingdom Now Theology: belief that the kingdom of God is established during this present era prior to Jesus' return.

leisure: free time from work.

ministry: "the act of serving" in evangelism, worship, or edification of believers; primarily helping to make faith a way of life for persons, communities, and cultures.

monasticism: relating to monks, nuns, and monasteries.

ontological: relating to the nature and relations of being or existence.

pneumatological: having to do with the Holy Spirit or the gifts of the Spirit.

postmillennialism: the belief that Christ's second coming will follow the millennium.

GLOSSARY

premillennialism: the belief that Christ's second coming will precede to the millennium.

providence: God sustaining and guiding humanity.

reconstructionist: one who ascribes to postmillennialism with emphasis of the Church taking dominion of society and establishing the kingdom of God prior to Jesus' return to reign.

remuneration: payment, wage, salary, or compensation for work done.

sacred: "includes all Church activities as well as work for the Church in the world such as community service in the name of the church, evangelism, teaching Sunday school, etc."[676]

secular: "anything not directly related to the Church."[677]

stewardship: the careful and responsible management of something entrusted to one's care.

theology of work: the study of "work" from God's perspective, especially as shown in the Bible.

vocation: a calling; God's call to a particular Christian role; the call of God to His Service; a person's career or profession.

work: paid employment; service rendered to another; any productive activity.

workaholic: "a person whose desire to work is compulsive, excessive, extreme."[678]

workplace leader: "anyone who leads or influences others in the workplace, even if he or she does not have a specific position of authority."[679]

workplace ministry: "an intentional focus of equipping men and women in all spheres of work and society to understand and experience their work life as a holy calling from God."[680]

ENDNOTES

INTRODUCTION

[1] Nancy R. Smith, *Workplace Spirituality: A Complete Guide for Business Leaders* (Peabody: Axial Age, 2006), xiii.

[2] David Hohne, "Work: The Big Picture," *The Briefing* 180, June 1996, under "Ecclesiastes: Solomon's Toil," accessed April 10, 2007, http://www.christiansatwork.org.uk/cgi-bin/caw.cgi?&page=resources&rescode=271.

[3] Miroslav Volf, "God at Work," *Word & World* 25, no. 4 (Fall 2005): 391-92.

[4] Most conservative theologians, such as George Ladd and Gerhard Hasel, agree that redemptive history (or "salvation history," *Heilsgeschichte*) is a unifying message or concept of the Bible, whereas Oscar Cullman is in the minority in taking it a step further and saying that salvation history is *the* unifying *center* of the Bible from which all other material can be organized. George Eldon Ladd, *A Theology of the New Testament*, rev. ed. edited by Donald A. Hagner (Grand Rapids: Wm. B. Eerdmans Publishing Co. 1993), 9, 21; Gerhard F. Hasel, *New Testament Theology: Basic Issues in the Current Debate* (Grand Rapids: Wm. B. Eerdmans Publishing Co. 1978), 148-49, 151, 153, 156, 203.

[5] Charles Ringma, "Tensions in a Theology of Work," July 1998, under "Doing Theology by Careful Listening and Reflection," accessed October 20, 2007, http://www.christiansatwork.org.uk/cgi-bin/caw.cgi?page=resources&rescode=233.

6. Robert J. Tamasy, introduction to *Jesus Works Here*, ed. Tamasy (Nashville: Broadman, 1995), 3.

CHAPTER 1

7. Pete R. Hammond, Paul Stevens, and Todd Svanoe, *The Marketplace Annotated Bibliography: A Christian Guide to Books on Work, Business & Vocation* (Downers Grove: IVP, 2002).
8. M. D. Chenu, *The Theology of Work: An Exploration*, (1963), trans. Lilian Soiron (Chicago: Regnery, 1966), originally published as *Pour une Theologie du Travail*, (Paris: Editions du Seuil, [1955]), 4.
9. Dorothy L. Sayers, "Why Work?" in *Creed or Chaos?* (1949; repr. Manchester: Sophia, 1974), 63.
10. Ibid. 64.
11. William H. Harrison, "Loving the Creation, Loving the Creator: Dorothy L. Sayers's Theology of Work," *Anglican Theological Review* 86, no. 2 (Spring 2004): 240, accessed September 28, 2006, http://search.ebscohost.com/login.aspx?direct=true&db=a9h&AN=13117223&site=ehost-live.
12. Ibid. 239.
13. Sayers, "Why Work?" 67.
14. Harrison, 241.
15. Josef Pieper, *Leisure, the Basis of Culture*, trans. Gerald Malsbary (1948; repr. South Bend: St. Augustine's, 1998).
16. Alistair Mackenzie, "Faith at Work: Vocation, the Theology of Work and the Pastoral Implications" (master's thesis, University of Otago, Dunedin, New Zealand, 1997), 42.
17. Pieper, 54.
18. J. H. Oldham, *Work in Modern Society* (1950; repr. Richmond: John Knox, 1962).
19. Hammond, Stevens, and Svanoe, 145.
20. Mackenzie, 34.
21. Oldham, 11.
22. Ibid. 49.
23. Alan Richardson, *The Biblical Doctrine of Work*, Ecumenical Biblical Studies no. 1 (1952; repr. London: SCM, 1954).
24. Mackenzie, 39.
25. Richardson, 17-18.
26. Ibid. 23.

[27] Karl Barth, *Church Dogmatics: III.4 The Doctrine of Creation*, ed. G. W. Bromiley and T. F. Torrance, trans. A. T. Mackay et al. (London: T & T Clark, 2004), Vol. 3, Part 4, originally published as *Die Kirchliche Dogmatick III: Die Lehre von der Schopfung 4*, (Zurich: Zollikon, 1951).

[28] Ibid. 473.

[29] Mackenzie, 44.

[30] Chenu, 23.

[31] Hammond, Stevens, and Svanoe, 54.

[32] Chenu, 8-9.

[33] Edwin G. Kaiser, *Theology of Work* (Westminster: Newman P, 1966).

[34] Gideon Goosen, *The Theology of Work*, Theology Today Series 22 (Hales Corners: Clergy Book Service, 1974).

[35] Ibid. 58.

[36] Ibid.

[37] Jacques Ellul, *The Ethics of Freedom*, trans. Geoffrey W. Bromiley (Grand Rapids: Eerdmans, 1976).

[38] Ibid. 496.

[39] Ibid.

[40] Ibid.

[41] Ibid. 495.

[42] Mackenzie, 59.

[43] Paul Marshall, "Vocation, Work, and Jobs," in *Labour of Love: Essays on Work*, by Paul Marshall et al. (Toronto: Wedge, 1980), 1-19.

[44] Ibid. 16.

[45] John Paul II, *Encyclical Letter on Human Work: Laborem Exercens*, trans. Vatican (Boston: Pauline, 1981).

[46] Leland Ryken, *Redeeming the Time: A Christian Approach to Work & Leisure* (Grand Rapids: Baker, 1995), 112.

[47] John Paul II, 23.

[48] Ibid. 5.

[49] Mackenzie, 60.

[50] Dorothee Soelle with Shirley A. Cloyes, *To Work and to Love: A Theology of Creation* (Philadelphia: Fortress, 1984).

[51] Mackenzie, 67.

[52] Soelle with Cloyes, 37.

[53] Doug Sherman and William Hendricks, *Your Work Matters to God* (1987; repr. Colorado Springs: NavPress, 1988).

54 Ibid. 77, 87.
55 M. Douglas Meeks, *God the Economist: The Doctrine of God and Political Economy* (Minneapolis: Fortress, 1989).
56 Ibid. 2, 181.
57 Ibid. 127-55.
58 Ibid. 133.
59 Lee Hardy, *The Fabric of this World: Inquiries into Calling, Career Choice, and the Design of Human Work* (Grand Rapids: Eerdmans, 1990).
60 Ibid. xv.
61 Miroslav Volf, *Work in the Spirit: Toward a Theology of Work* (1991; repr. Eugene: Wipf, 2001).
62 Ibid. 79.
63 Ibid. 107-09.
64 Ibid. 110.
65 Ibid. 123.
66 Hammond, Stevens, and Svanoe, 158.
67 Gary D. Badcock, *The Way of Life: A Theology of Christian Vocation* (Eugene: Wipf, 2002).
68 Ibid. 141.
69 Ibid. 142.
70 Ibid. 141.
71 R. Paul Stevens, *The Other Six Days: Vocation, Work, and Ministry in Biblical Perspective* (Grand Rapids: Eerdmans, 2000; Vancouver, BC: Regent College, 2000), repr. of *The Abolition of the Laity* (1999).
72 Ibid. 89, 97-98.
73 Alistair Mackenzie and Wayne Kirkland, *Where's God on Monday? Integrating Faith and Work Every Day of the Week* (Colorado Springs: NavPress, 2003).
74 Ibid. 18-20.
75 Armand Larive, *After Sunday: A Theology of Work* (New York: Continuum, 2004).
76 Ibid. 72-73.
77 Jozef D. Zalot, review of *After Sunday: A Theology of Work*, by Armand Larive. *Theological Studies* 66, no. 3 (2005): 718, accessed September 28, 2006, http://search.ebscohost.com/login.aspx?direct=true&db=aph&AN=18032281&site=ehost-live.

[78] Fredrica Harris Thompsett, review of *After Sunday: A Theology of Work*, by Armand Larive. *Anglican Theological Review* 87, no. 4 (2004): 704, accessed September 28, 2006, http://www.epnet.com.
[79] Douglas J. Schuurman, *Vocation: Discerning Our Callings in Life* (Grand Rapids: Eerdmans, 2004).
[80] Ibid. 180.
[81] Ibid. xii.
[82] Darrell Cosden, *A Theology of Work: Work and the New Creation* (Eugene: Wipf, 2005).
[83] Ibid. 178-85.
[84] Darrell Cosden, *The Heavenly Good of Earthly Work* (United Kingdom: Paternoster P, 2006; Peabody: Hendrickson, 2006).
[85] Ibid. 2.
[86] Ibid.
[87] David H. Jensen, *Responsive Labor: A Theology of Work* (Louisville: Westminster, 2006).
[88] Ibid. x.
[89] Jensen, ix.
[90] Will Messenger, exec ed. *Theology of Work Bible Commentary*, One Volume Edition (Peabody: Hendrickson Publishers Marketing, 2016), back cover.
[91] Theology of Work Project, "About," Theology of Work Project, accessed November 27, 2020, https://www.theologyofwork.org/about.
[92] Os Hillman, Faith@Work: What Every Pastor and Church Leader Should Know (Cumming: Aslan, 2004), 211-23.
[93] Peter C. Wagner, *The Church in the Workplace* (Ventura: Regal, 2006), 9.
[94] Ibid. 16.
[95] Ibid. 110.
[96] Ibid. 16.
[97] Ibid. 110-12.
[98] Os Hillman, *Faith & Work: Do They Mix?* (Alpharetta: Aslan, 2000).
[99] Hillman, *Faith@Work: What Every Pastor and Church Leader Should Know*.
[100] Os Hillman, *The 9 to 5 Window* (Ventura: Regal, 2005).
[101] Kent Humphreys, *Lasting Investments: A Pastor's Guide for Equipping Workplace Leaders to Leave a Spiritual Legacy* (Colorado Springs: NavPress, 2004).

[102] Kent Humphreys, *Shepherding Horses: Understanding God's Plan for Transforming Leaders* (Oklahoma City: Triad Marketing, 2006).
[103] Ibid. 1-9.
[104] Linda Rios Brook, *Frontline Christians in a Bottom-Line World* (Shippensburg: Destiny, 2004), 30-31.
[105] Ibid. 28.
[106] Ibid. 31, 35-36.
[107] Ibid. 18-27.
[108] Ibid. 207.
[109] David W. Miller, *God at Work: The History and Promise of the Faith at Work Movement* (New York: Oxford UP, 2007).
[110] Ibid. 126-42.
[111] Will Messenger, exec ed. *Calling and Work*, The Bible and Your Work Study Series (Peabody: Hendrickson Publishers Marketing, 2015), viii.
[112] Will Messenger, exec ed. *Genesis 1-11*, The Bible and Your Work Study Series (Peabody: Hendrickson Publishers Marketing, 2015), viii.

CHAPTER 2

[113] Carly Friesen, "Labor: Sin or Sacrament?" *Direction* 10 (1981): 5, accessed January 10, 2007, http://www.directionjournal.org/article/?411.
[114] Otto J. Helweg, "The Secular and Sacred: Friends or Foes?" under "Theological Background," accessed February 12, 2007, http://www.leaderu.com/offices/o_helweg/secular_or_sacred.html.
[115] David Pawson, "Work," Leadership Development Seminar, August 26, 1993, Audiocassette, Asia Full Gospel Business Men's Fellowship International Convention, Hong Kong Convention Center, Hong Kong.
[116] Ibid.
[117] C. J. Mahaney, *Why Work?* Quest Tape of the Month, QT161, Audiocassette, [Washington D.C.] 1991.
[118] Ibid.
[119] Hillman, *The 9 to 5 Window*, 84.
[120] Chenu, 2.
[121] Ibid. 2-4.

ENDNOTES

[122] Seward Hiltner, "Needed: A New Theology of Work," *Theology Today* 31, no. 3 (October 1974): 247, accessed September 28, 2006, http://search.ebscohost.com/login.aspx?direct=true&db=rfh&AN=ATLA0000748108&site=ehost-live.

[123] Keith Harper, review of *Work in the Spirit: Toward a Theology of Work*, by Miroslav Volf, *Journal of the Evangelical Theological Society* 36 (September 1993): 386, accessed September 28, 2006, http://search.ebscohost.com/login.aspx?direct=true&db=rfh&AN=ATLA0000282041&site=ehost-live.

[124] Volf, *Work in the Spirit*, 69.

[125] Curtis Chang, "Work as Sacrament," June 4, 2004, 2, accessed February 11, 2007, http://www.the-river.org/resources/Work-as-sacrament.pdf.

[126] Jim Lewis, "A Theology of Work," The Witness, 2003, 1, accessed March 9, 2007, http://www.thewitness.org/generalconvention03/TheologyOfWork.ps-.pdf.

[127] Larvine, 7.

[128] Os Hillman and Angie Hillman, *Called to the Workplace—From Esau to Joseph: Living for a Cause Greater Than Ourselves*, Workshop Workbook, [Marketplace Leaders, c. 2005], 2.

[129] Os Hillman, *God in the Workplace*, DVD, (FaithAndWorkResources.com, 2005).

[130] Miller, *God at Work*, 101.

[131] Theology of Work Project, "Theology of Work," Theology of Work Project, accessed October 2, 2008, http://www.theologyofwork.org; Haddon W. Robinson, foreword to *Theology of Work Bible Commentary*, One Volume edition, edited by Will Messenger (Peabody: Hendrickson Publishers Marketing, 2016), xxviii.

[132] Theology of Work Project, "Theology of Work Project," Theology of Work Project, accessed November 27, 2020, http://www.theologyofwork.org.

CHAPTER 3

[133] Ryken, 71.

[134] Glenn Bryan, "The Value of Work: A Case for Promoting Christian Service Opportunities to College Students," May 1991, under "Historical Evolution of Attitudes toward Work," accessed January 11,

2007, http://www.cccu.org/resourcecenter/resID.854,parentCatID.89/rc_detail.asp.
[135] Ryken, 72.
[136] Friesen, 3.
[137] Hardy, 8-9.
[138] Goosen, 18-20.
[139] Pawson.
[140] Ryken, 85, 87.
[141] Kaiser, 37.
[142] Goosen, 23.
[143] Ibid. 3.
[144] Richardson, 22.
[145] Goosen, 25.
[146] Ibid. 31.
[147] Merrill C. Tenney, *New Testament Survey*, rev. ed. by Walter M. Dunnett (1985; repr. Grand Rapids: Eerdmans, 1996; Leicester, England: IVP, 1996), 97.
[148] With reference to the Greek word translated "tentmaker" in Acts 18:3, Todd D. Still says that most scholars now say that Paul was "a leatherworker who crafted leather products, including tents" instead of "a weaver who made tentcloth from *cilicium* (i.e. goats' hair)": Todd D. Still, "Did Paul Loathe Manual Labor? Revisiting the Work of Ronald F. Hock on the Apostle's Tentmaking and Social Class," *Journal of Biblical Literature* 125, no. 4 (Winter 2006): 781.
[149] Daniel R. Haskins and Yvonne Smith, "Christians in Strategic Leadership: Towards an Integration of Faith and the Top Management Team," October 30, 2004, accessed March 29, 2007, http://www.cbfa.org/papers/2004conf/Haskins-Smith.doc, 11.
[150] Mackenzie, 184.
[151] Kaiser, 110.
[152] Paul Marshall, 7.
[153] Richard Higginson, "Worldly Vocation: An Historical Overview," [c. 2000,] under "Vita active, vita contemplativa," accessed March 29, 2007, http://www.christiansatwork.org.uk/cgi-bin/caw.cgi?&page=resources&rescode=268.
[154] Lee J. Smith, "A Biblical Theology of Work," [c. 2002,] under "I. A Short History of Attitudes about Work in Western Civilizations,"

accessed February 11, 2007, http://www.randolphefree.org/monographtheowork.htm.

[155] Bryan, under "Historical Evolution of Attitudes toward Work."

[156] Mackenzie and Kirkland, 83.

[157] Os Guinness, *The Call: Finding and Fulfilling the Central Purpose of Your Life* (Nashville: W Publishing, 2003), 31-32.

[158] Friesen, 6-7.

[159] Robert L. Calhoun, "Work and Vocation in Christian History," in *Work and Vocation: A Christian Discussion*, ed. John Oliver Nelson (New York: Harper, 1954), 99.

[160] Ibid.

[161] Ibid.

[162] Ibid. 103.

[163] Oldham, 45.

[164] Ryken, 75.

[165] Higginson, under "Martin Luther."

[166] Goosen, 64.

[167] Stephen J. Nichols, *Martin Luther: A Guided Tour of His Life and Thought* (Phillipsburg: P&R, 2002), 84.

[168] Oldham, 45.

[169] Chuck Colson and Jack Eckerd, *Why America Doesn't Work* (Dallas: Word, 1991), 36.

[170] D. Michael Bennethum, *Listen! God is Calling! Luther Speaks of Vocation, Faith, and Work* (Minneapolis: Augsburg Fortress, 2003), 52.

[171] Goosen, 63-64.

[172] Colson and Eckerd, 37.

[173] H. Richard Niebuhr, *Christ and Culture* (New York: HarperCollins, 1951), 217-18.

[174] Wagner, 36.

[175] J. I. Packer, *A Quest for Godliness: The Puritan Vision of the Christian Life* (1990; repr. Wheaton: Crossway, 1994), 23-24.

[176] Ryken, 109.

[177] Lee Smith, under "I. A Short History of Attitudes about Work in Western Civilization."

[178] Colson and Eckerd, 39.

CHAPTER 4

[179] Robert P. Imbelli, review of *Callings: Twenty Centuries of Christian Wisdom on Vocation*, ed. William C. Placher, *Commonweal* 133, no. 5 (2006): 32. accessed September 28, 2006, http://search.ebscohost.com/login.aspx?direct=true&db=vah&AN=CPLI0000424241&site=ehost-live.

[180] Guinness, 38-39.

[181] Ryken, 77.

[182] Lee J. Smith, "A Biblical Theology of Work," [c. 2002,] under "I. A Short History of Attitudes about Work in Western Civilization," accessed February 11, 2007, http://www.randolphefree.org/monographtheowork.htm.

[183] Ryken, 79.

[184] Goosen, 56.

[185] John A. Bernbaum and Simon M. Steer, *Why Work? Careers and Employment in Biblical Perspective* (Grand Rapids: Baker, 1986), 30.

[186] Ryken, 80.

[187] Dorothy L. Sayers, *Are Women Human?* (1971; repr. Grand Rapids: Eerdmans, 2005), 32.

[188] Ibid. 61-62.

[189] Ibid. 32.

[190] Ibid. 33.

[191] Laura K. Simmons, *Creed without Chaos: Exploring Theology in the Writings of Dorothy L. Sayers* (Grand Rapids: Baker, 2005), 173.

[192] Simmons, 176.

[193] Wagner, 37.

[194] Ibid.

[195] Ibid.

[196] Ibid.

[197] Ibid.

[198] Pawson.

[199] Ibid.

[200] Mark Greene, "The Great Divide—the Greatest Cultural Challenge Facing the Church," [c. 2000,] under "The Great Divide," accessed March 29, 2007, http://www.intheworkplace.com/articles_view.asp?articleid=12831&columnid=1935.

[201] A.W. Tozer, *The Pursuit of God* (Harrisburg: Christian, 1948), 127.

[202] James M. Roseman, "Toward a Theology of Work and Business: Reflections on Christianity, Calling, and Commerce," October 3, 2003, 10-15, http://www.dbu.edu/naugle/pdf/Towards1.pdf (October 20, 2007).

[203] John D. Beckett, *Loving Monday: Succeeding in Business without Selling Your Soul*, expanded ed. (1998; repr, Downers Grove: IVP, 2006), 69.

[204] Mahaney.

[205] Ryken, 56.

[206] Patrick T. Reardon, "Good Job!" *U.S. Catholic* 68, no. 9 (September 2003): 50.

[207] Mahaney.

CHAPTER 5

[208] M. D. Geldard, "Work," in *Encyclopedia of Biblical & Christian Ethics*, rev. ed. ed. R. K. Harrison (Nashville: Thomas Nelson, 1992), 444.

[209] Stevens, 107.

[210] Paul S. Minear, "Work and Vocation in Scripture," in *Work and Vocation: A Christian Discussion*, ed. John Oliver Nelson (New York: Harper, 1954), 44.

[211] Robert J. Banks, *God the Worker: Journeys into the Mind, Heart and Imagination of God*, North American ed. (1992; repr. Valley Forge: Judson, 1994).

[212] John Paul II, 5.

[213] *Where We Stand: The Official Position Papers of the Assemblies of God*, (Springfield: Gospel, 2003), 106.

[214] Harrison, 251-52.

[215] Dorothy L. Sayers, *The Mind of the Maker*, (1941; repr. New York: HarperCollins, 1979), 22.

[216] Peter Stuart, "Christians in the Workplace: A Practical Theology of Work," Latimer Occasional Paper No. 6. (Christchurch, New Zealand: Latimer Fellowship. Nov. 2000), 3, accessed April 7, 2007, http://www.latimer.org.nz/downloads/theology-work.pdf.

[217] Harrison, 252.

[218] Reardon, 50.

[219] Richardson, 24.

[220] Julian Doorey, "Faith in the Work Place," *Reality Magazine* 38, 2000, under "'Added Value Work' by Humans," accessed February 11, 2007, http://www.reality.org.nz/articles/38/38-doorey.html.

[221] Mackenzie and Kirkland, 19.

[222] Thoralf Gilbrant, ed. *The Old Testament Hebrew-English Dictionary*, vol. 7 of *The Complete Biblical Library: The Old Testament Hebrew-English Dictionary*, ed. Thoralf Gilbrant (Springfield: World Library, 2000), 340.

[223] Sherman and Hendricks, 82.

[224] Stanley M. Horton, *The Old Testament Study Bible: Genesis*, vol. 1 of *The Complete Biblical Library: The Old Testament*, ed. Thoralf Gilbrant (Springfield: World Library, 1994), 29.

[225] Mackenzie, 57.

[226] John H. Sailhamer, "Genesis," in vol. 7 of *The Expositor's Bible Commentary*, ed. Frank E. Gaebelein (Grand Rapids: Zondervan, 1990), 45.

[227] Gordon P. Hugenberger, "Is Work the Result of the Fall? A Note on Genesis 2:15," (Sept. 2002), 2-9, accessed February 11, 2007, http://www.parkstreet.org/pulpit/Work-Genesis2.pdf.

[228] Geldard, 443.

[229] Richardson, 29.

[230] Horton, 39.

[231] Goosen, 65-66.

[232] Oldham, 50.

[233] Harrison, 255.

[234] Mackenzie, 57.

[235] Sailhamer, 45.

[236] Ellul, 496.

[237] Raymond O. Bystrom, "God as Worker: How it Affects Life and Ministry," *Direction* 32, no. 2 (Fall 2003): 168, 171n8, accessed February 11, 2007, http://www.directionjournal.org/article/?1306.

[238] Richardson, 28-29.

[239] Wayne Kirkland, "God's Co-workers," *Reality Magazine* 38, 2000, under "Developing a more biblical view of work," accessed April 7, 2007, http://www.reality.org.nz/articles/38/38-kirkland.html.

[240] Mackenzie and Kirkland, 28.

[241] Rich Lusk, "God and Work, Part 2: God Working Through Us, God Working Against Us (Col. 3:22-24; 2 Thess. 3:6-13; Prov. 6:6-11)"

[241] (sermon, Trinity Presbyterian Church, Birmingham, AL, June 5, 2005), Trinity Presbyterian Church Sermon Index, MP3 Audio file, accessed March 29, 2007, http://www.trinity-pres.net/audio/sermon05-06-05.mp3.

[242] Ibid.

[243] Mackenzie and Kirkland, 28.

[244] Richardson, 28.

[245] Donald J. Isaac, "Work and Christian Calling," *Direction* 32 (2003): 186, accessed April 11, 2007, http://www.directionjournal.org/article/?1308.

[246] Gordon Kirk, "A Theology of Work: Our Work as an Aspect of our Worship" (sermon, Lake Avenue Church, Pasadena, CA, August 1, 2004), LAC Sermons Online, Real Audio file, accessed April 7, 2007, http://www.lakeavefamily.org/audio/wc/2004/20040801wc.rm.

[247] Mahaney.

[248] Hohne, under "From Dominion to Toil."

[249] Ibid.

[250] David J. Bosch, *Transforming Mission: Paradigm Shifts in Theology of Mission*, American Society of Missiology Ser. 16, 1991 (Maryknoll: Orbis, 2005), xv.

[251] Miller, *God at Work*, 24-25.

[252] Bill Hammon, *The Day of the Saints: Equipping Believers for Their Revolutionary Role in Ministry* (2002; repr. Shippensburg: Destiny, 2003), 410; Bosch, 315; Miller, *God at Work*, 26.

[253] Bosch, 318.

[254] Hammon, 227.

[255] Miller, *God at Work*, 41.

[256] Ibid. 42.

[257] Hammon, 227.

[258] John F. Walvoord, *The Revelation of Jesus Christ* (1966; repr. Chicago: Moody, 1978), 305.

[259] Ibid. 311.

[260] J. Dwight Pentecost, *Things to Come: A Study in Biblical Eschatology* (1958; repr. Grand Rapids: Zondervan.1977), 561.

[261] Herman A. Hoyt, *The End Times* (1969; repr. Winona Lake: BMH, 1995), 224.

[262] W. A. Criswell, *Expository Sermons on Revelation: Five Volumes Complete and Unabridged in One* (Grand Rapids: Zondervan, 1966), 5:106.
[263] Ibid. 5:106-07.
[264] Ibid. 5:112.
[265] Andrew McDearmid, *Eschatology: A Study Guide*, 1980 (Irving: ICI UP, 1995), 181.
[266] Volf, *Work in the Spirit*, 89.
[267] Ibid. 91.
[268] Goosen, 75.
[269] Roseman, 13.
[270] Goosen, 74.
[271] Mark Oppenheimer, "Miroslav Volf Spans Conflicting Worlds," 2003, under "Miroslav Volf Spans Conflicting Worlds," accessed April 11, 2007, http://www.religion-online.org/showarticle.asp?title=2688, repr. of *The Christian Century*, January 11, 2003, 18-23.
[272] Cosden, *Heavenly Good of Earthly Work*, 2.
[273] Ibid.
[274] Ibid. 33.
[275] Ibid. 53.
[276] Ibid. 114-15.
[277] Kirk, "A Theology of Work: Our Work as an Aspect of our Worship."
[278] Goosen, 75.
[279] Ibid.
[280] Hoyt, 241.
[281] John Jefferson Davis, "Will There Be New Work in the New Creation?" *Evangelical Review of Theology* 31, no. 3 (July 2007): 258.
[282] Ibid.
[283] Ibid. 257.
[284] Ibid, 259.
[285] Ibid, 260.
[286] Ibid.
[287] Ibid, 261.
[288] Ibid.
[289] Ibid, 262.
[290] Ibid.
[291] Pentecost, 561.

[292] Ibid, 552.
[293] Dave Hunt, *Whatever Happened to Heaven?* (Eugene: Harvest, 1988), 305.
[294] Ibid, 307.
[295] Ibid, 308.
[296] Pentecost, 562.
[297] Ibid, 582.
[298] Mahaney.
[299] Criswell, 5:132.
[300] Ibid.
[301] Walvoord, 331.
[302] Hoyt, 241.
[303] Ibid, 242.

CHAPTER 6

[304] Rick Warren, *The Purpose Driven Life: What on Earth am I Here For?* (Grand Rapids: Zondervan, 2002), 67.
[305] Lee Smith, under "5. As Christians our work has significant purposes."
[306] Hillman, *Faith@Work: What Every Pastor and Church Leader Should Know*, 44.
[307] Oldham, 51.
[308] Ibid.
[309] Sherman and Hendricks, 53.
[310] Stuart, 4-5.
[311] Pawson; Hardy, 174.
[312] Lee Smith, under "5. As Christians our work has significant purposes."
[313] James Davidson, "Why Work? Or 5 Reasons to Get out of Bed on Monday Morning." [July 1996], under "5. To support gospel workers," accessed April 9, 2007, http://www.christiansatwork.org.uk/cgi-bin/caw.cgi?&page=resources&rescode=273.
[314] Mark Greene, *Thank God it's Monday: Ministry in the Workplace*, 3rd ed. (2001; repr. Bletchley, Eng.: Scripture Union, 2003), 15.
[315] William Carr Peel and Walt Larimore, *Going Public with Your Faith: Becoming a Spiritual Influence at Work* (Grand Rapids: Zondervan, 2003), 64-74.
[316] Sherman and Hendricks, 66-72; Roseman, 6.

[317] Robert S. Rayburn, "Series Introduction: No. 3: The Creation Mandate (Genesis 1:26-28)," Theology of Work Ser. Rec. April 9, 2006, Faith Presbyterian Church, Tacoma, WA.

[318] Carol L. Haywood, "Does Our Theology of Work Need Reworking?" *Currents in Theology and Mission* 8 (October 1981): 299, accessed September 28, 2006, http://search.ebscohost.com/login.aspx?direct=true&db=rfh&AN=ATLA0000786949&site=ehost-live.

[319] Lee Smith, under "5. As Christians our work has significant purposes."

CHAPTER 7

[320] Ryken, 214.

[321] Anglican Church Dioceses of Sydney, "50/95 Theology of Work," 1999, under "Background," accessed February 12, 2007, http://www.sydney.anglican.asn.au/synod/synod99/work.html.

[322] Arthur Wallis, foreword to *Serving Christ in the Workplace: Secular Work is Full-Time Service*. By Larry Peabody (Fort Washington: CLC, 2004; repr. of *Secular Work is Full-time Service*. 1974), 8.

[323] Hillman, *The 9 to 5 Window*, 20.

[324] Ryken, 76.

[325] Daniel R. Haskins and Yvonne Smith, "Christians in Strategic Leadership: Towards an Integration of Faith and the Top Management Team," October 30, 2004, 13, accessed March 29, 2007, http://www.cbfa.org/papers/2004conf/Haskins-Smith.doc.

[326] Lusk.

[327] Gustaf Wingren, *Luther on Vocation*, trans. Carl C. Rasmussen (Eugene: Wipf, 1957), 2.

[328] Friesen, 8.

[329] Frederick J. Gaiser, "What Luther *Didn't* Say about Vocation," *Word & World* 25, no. 4 (Fall 2005): 360.

[330] Higginson, under "Martin Luther."

[331] Ryken, 192.

[332] Bryan, under "The Biblical Ideal of Work."

[333] Ryken, 193.

[334] Anglican Church Dioceses of Sydney, under "When is the Obligation to Work Superseded?"

[335] Ryken, 193.

[336] Ibid.

[337] Ibid.

ENDNOTES

[338] Richardson, 38.
[339] Wingren, 1.
[340] Ryken, 195.
[341] Ibid.
[342] Gordon D. Fee, *The First Epistle to the Corinthians*, vol. of *The International Commentary on the New Testament* (Grand Rapids: Eerdmans, 1987), 307.
[343] Hardy, 47.
[344] Lee Smith, under "6. God is the one who gives us the abilities, opportunities and the successes we enjoy."
[345] Wingren, 1.
[346] Richardson, 35.
[347] Paul Marshall, 13.
[348] Richardson, 35.
[349] Ibid. 36.
[350] Ellul, 496.
[351] Barth, 472.
[352] Ellul, 495.
[353] Ibid.
[354] Ibid. 506-07.
[355] Volf, 109.
[356] Schuurman, 180.
[357] Darrell Cosden, *The Heavenly Good of Earthly Work*, 41.
[358] Stuart McGregor, "Thy Workmate is Thy Neighbor: Essay on the Theology of Work," 2002, 4, accessed April 11, 2006, http://www.definitive.co.nz/essay/worktheologyresponse.pdf.
[359] Ryken, 194.
[360] William C. Placher, introduction to *Callings: Twenty Centuries of Christian Wisdom on Vocation*, by Placher, ed. (Grand Rapids: Eerdmans, 2005), 5.
[361] Ryken, 194.
[362] Kathryn Kleinhans, "The Work of a Christian: Vocation in Lutheran Perspective," *Word & World* 25, no. 4 (Fall 2005): 396.
[363] Ibid.
[364] Matt. 6:11.
[365] Wayne Grudem, *Systematic Theology: An Introduction to Biblical Doctrine* (Grand Rapids: Zondervan Publishing House, 1994), 320.
[366] Ibid. 398.

[367] Ibid.
[368] Ryken, 194.
[369] Hardy, xiv-xvii.
[370] Ryken, 200.
[371] Kleinhans, 396.
[372] McGregor, 6.
[373] Kleinhans, 399.
[374] Ibid.
[375] Pawson.
[376] Gene Edward Veith, Jr. *God at Work: Your Christian Vocation in All of Life* (Wheaton: Crossway, 2002), 162.
[377] Higginson, under "Martin Luther."
[378] Haskins and Smith, 14-15.
[379] Volf, 107-09.
[380] Higginson, under "Volf's Critique of Work as Vocation."
[381] Oppenheimer, under "Miroslav Volf Spans Conflicting Worlds."
[382] James C. Davidson and David P. Caddell, "Religion and the Meaning of Work," *Journal for the Scientific Study of Religion* 33, no. 2 (1994): 145.
[383] Higginson, under "Volf's Critique of Work as Vocation."
[384] Ibid. under "Is Gift Enough?"
[385] Will Messenger, *Calling and Work*, 36.
[386] Hardy, 66.
[387] Sayers, "Why Work?" 73.
[388] Sayers, "Why Work?" 74.
[389] Ibid. 71.
[390] Ibid. 78.
[391] Sherman and Hendricks, 143.
[392] Helweg, under "5. Christ of culture (liberal)."
[393] Hardy, 63.
[394] Wagner, 107.
[395] Ed Silvoso, *Anointed for Business* (Ventura: Regal, 2002), 34.
[396] Will Messenger, *Calling and Work*, 26.
[397] Volf, 122.
[398] Ibid.
[399] Os Hillman, *Are You a Biblical Worker?* (Cumming: Aslan, 2003), 7.
[400] Hammon, 269-70.
[401] Wagner, 117.

[402] Ibid. 111-12, 163; Rich Marshall with Ken Walker, *God@Work Volume 2: Developing Ministers in the Marketplace* (Shippensburg: Destiny, 2005), 70; Hillman, *The 9 to 5 Window*, 147; Hammon, 251; Brook, 180-81.
[403] *Where We Stand*, 294-95.
[404] Ibid. 298.
[405] Ibid.
[406] Oppenheimer, under "Miroslav Volf Spans Conflicting Worlds."
[407] Kleinhans, 399.
[408] Ed Zabocki, "A Theology of Work for Changing Times," [c. 2000,] under "Now," accessed April 11, 2007, http://www.nafra-sfo.org/work_commission_resources/wrkart10.html.
[409] Hillman, *The 9 to 5 Window*, 134.

CHAPTER 8

[410] Richardson, 53.
[411] Pawson.
[412] Hohne, under "Proverbs: Solomon's Dominion."
[413] Bernard Rossier, "Verse-by-Verse Commentary on Ephesians, Philippians, Colossians, Philemon." *The New Testament Study Bible: Galatians-Philemon*, vol. 8 of *The Complete Biblical Library*, ed. Thoralf Gilbrant, 16 vols. (Springfield: Complete Biblical Library, 1989), 165.
[414] Richardson, 41.
[415] Pawson.
[416] Andy Stanley, "Part 1: Meet the Boss," *Taking Care of Business: Finding God at Work*, DVD (North Point Ministries, Inc. 2005).
[417] Ibid.
[418] Ibid.
[419] Ibid.
[420] Gordon Kirk, "A Theology of Work: An Encouragement to Employees," (sermon delivered at Lake Avenue Church, Pasadena, CA, July 17, 2004), LAC Sermons Online, Real Audio file, accessed April 7, 2007, http://www.lakeavefamily.org/audio/wc/2004/20040717wc.rm.
[421] Ibid.
[422] Will Messenger, *Theology of Work Bible Commentary*, 832.
[423] Ibid. 833.

424 Kirk.
425 Hillman, *The 9 to 5 Window*, 52.
426 Richardson, 64.
427 Ibid. 49.
428 Lee Smith, under "8. There are a number of characteristics and attitudes which should characterize our work."
429 Reardon, 50.
430 Kirk, "A Theology of Work: An Encouragement to Employees."
431 Rossier, 279, also makes this point.
432 Samuel J. Schultz, "Verse-by-Verse Commentary on Obadiah, Micha, Haggai, Zechariah, Malachi." *The Old Testament Study Bible: Daniel-Malachi*, vol. 15 of *The Complete Biblical Library: The Old Testament*, ed. Thoralf Gilbrant, 15 vols. (Springfield: Complete Biblical Library, 1999), 631.

CHAPTER 9

433 Sherman and Hendricks, 207.
434 Mahaney.
435 John A. Bernbaum and Simon M. Steer, *Why Work? Careers and Employment in Biblical Perspective* (Grand Rapids: Baker, 1986), 3.
436 Mahaney.
437 Ibid.
438 Pawson.
439 Bryan, under "The Contemporary Response to Work."
440 Ryken, 192.
441 Lee Smith, under "7. Work is not to become an idol."
442 Pat Gelsinger, *Balancing Your Family, Faith & Work* (Colorado Springs: Life Journey—Cook Communications, 2003), 121-22.
443 Ted W. Engstrom and David J. Juroe, *The Work Trap* (Old Tappan: Revell, 1979), 198-99.
444 Ibid. 192-95.
445 Ibid. 203.
446 Ryken, 165.
447 Mackenzie and Kirkland, 60.
448 Ryken, 28.
449 Mackenzie and Kirkland, 53.
450 Ryken, 171.
451 Sayers, "Why Work?" 75.

ENDNOTES

[452] Richardson, 53.
[453] Ryken, 189.
[454] Robert S. Rayburn, "Retirement (Eccles. 12:1-5)," Theology of Work Ser. Rec. June 4, 2006 (Faith Presbyterian Church, Tacoma, WA).
[455] Mahaney.
[456] Rayburn, "Retirement (Eccles. 12:1-5)."
[457] Lee Smith, under "4. What about retirement?"
[458] Andy Mills, *Part 2: God's Vision for Work*, audio file, 2014, https://soundcloud.com/theology-of-work/part-2-gods-vision-for-work-1.

CHAPTER 10

[459] Robert Barnett, "An Outline of Theological Reflections on the Purpose of Work," December 2003, 1-7, accessed December 15, 2006, http://www.gordonconwell.edu/ockenga/mockler/RBarnett_OutlineTheolWork.pdf.
[460] Ringma, under "Doing Theology by Careful Listening and Reflection."
[461] Goosen, 67.
[462] Ringma, under "Doing Theology by Careful Listening and Reflection."
[463] Goosen, 69.
[464] Roseman, 10-15.
[465] Ibid.
[466] Miller, *God at Work*, 126-42.
[467] David W. Miller, "The Sunday-Monday Gap: Called to Pew and Profit," January 6, 2005, under "The Four Es," accessed February 14, 2007, http://www.yale.edu/faith/esw/x_miller_pewandprofit.html.
[468] Miller, *God at Work*, 11.

CHAPTER 11

[469] Miller, "The Sunday-Monday Gap: Called to Pew and Profit," under "Faith at Work."
[470] Michael McLoughlin, "A New Way to Work: A Paradigm Shift for Marketplace Mission in the 21st Century," [c. 2005,] under "A New Way to Work," accessed February 21, 2007, http://www .intheworkplace.com/articles_view.asp?articleid=12874&columnid=1935.

[471] Pete Hammond, "Faith at Work is More than Witnessing," November 5, 2004, InterVarsity, under "Faith at Work is More than Witnessing," accessed February 21, 2007, http://www.intervarsity.org/news/news.php?item_id=1411.

[472] Miller, *God at Work*, 4.

[473] Ibid. 123.

[474] Nancy R. Smith, *Workplace Spirituality*, xvii.

[475] Ibid. 8.

[476] Ibid. 9.

[477] Ibid.

[478] Miller, "The Sunday-Monday Gap: Called to Pew and Profit" under "Faith at Work."

[479] Hammond, "Faith at Work is More than Witnessing."

[480] Mike McLoughlin et al. comp. and eds. *2003 – 2004 International Faith and Work Directory* (Cumming: Aslan, 2003), 6.

[481] Hillman, *The 9 to 5 Window*, 85.

[482] Ibid. 84.

[483] Ibid. 82.

[484] Wagner, 76.

[485] Vinson Synan, *Under His Banner: History of Full Gospel Business Men's Fellowship International* (Costa Mesa: Gift, 1992), 38.

[486] Ibid. 39.

[487] Ibid.

[488] Ibid.

[489] Hillman, *Faith@Work: What Every Pastor and Church Leader Should Know*, 1.

[490] Robert J. Tamasy, *Marketplace Ambassadors: CBMC's Continuing Legacy of Evangelism and Disciplemaking* (Chattanooga: Christian Business Men's Connection, 2019), 49.

[491] Hillman, *Faith@Work*, 2.

[492] Edith L. Blumhofer, *The Assemblies of God: A Chapter in the Story of American Pentecostalism*, Vol. 2-Since 1941 (Springfield: Gospel Publishing House, 1989), 89.

[493] Demos Shakarian, with John Sherrill and Elizabeth Sherrill, *The Happiest People on Earth* (Chappaqua: Steward Press, 1975), 122.

[494] David R. Enlow, *Men Aflame: The Story of CBMC, 1930 – 1965* (1962; repr. Chattanooga: CBMC, 2019), 125.

[495] Wagner, 78.

ENDNOTES

[496] Ibid. 78-79.
[497] William W. Menzies, *Anointed to Serve* (Springfield: Gospel Publishing House, 1971), 338.
[498] J. R. Zeigler, "Full Gospel Business Men's Fellowship International," *The New International Dictionary of Pentecostal and Charismatic Movements*, ed. Stanley M. Burgess, rev. and exp. ed. (Grand Rapids: Zondervan, 2002), 653.
[499] Synan, 61.
[500] Wagner, 79.
[501] Hillman, *The 9 to 5 Window*, 80-81.
[502] Wagner, 75.
[503] Hillman, *The 9 to 5 Window*, 81-82.

CHAPTER 12

[504] Enlow, 7.
[505] CBMC, "CBMC," accessed April 12, 2020, https://www.cbmc.com.
[506] CBMC, "Our Mission", accessed April 12, 2020, https://www.cbmc.com/mission.
[507] Enlow, 7.
[508] Tamasy, *Marketplace Ambassadors*, 13.
[509] Enlow. 47.
[510] Ibid. 113.
[511] Ibid. 125; Tamasy, *Marketplace Ambassadors*, 19.
[512] Tamasy, *Marketplace Ambassadors*, 133-34.
[513] Ibid.
[514] Ibid. 134-35.
[515] Tamasy, *Marketplace Ambassadors*, 86.
[516] CBMC Kenya, "CBMC Kenya," accessed April 12, 2020, https://cbmckenya.co.ke/; Korea CBMC of North America, "About KCBMC," accessed April 12, 2020, https://en.kcbmc.net/about-kcbmc/.
[517] CBMC International, "Donate Now | CBMC International," accessed April 12, 2020, https://www.cbmcint.com/donate/.
[518] CBMC International, "CBMC International 2016 Ministry Report", accessed April 12, 2020, http://www.cbmcint.com/wp-content/uploads/2016/08/CBMC-Annual-Report-2016.pdf; CBMC International, "CBMC International 2018 Ministry Report",

accessed April 12, 2020, https://www.cbmcint.com/wp-content/uploads/2018/08/CBMC_Ministry_Report_Web2018.pdf.
[519] Bill McAvinney-Woolley, interview, May 29, 2020.
[520] CBMC, "The History of CBMC," CBMC: A Movement of Men, accessed January 28, 2007, http://www.cbmc.com/about/history.aspx.
[521] Tamasy, *Marketplace Ambassadors*, 136.
[522] CBMC International, "CBMC International 2018 Ministry Report."
[523] Synan, 12.
[524] Lee Braxton, "A Dream Comes True." *Voice*, February 1953.
[525] Synan, 11.
[526] Shakarian, Sherrill, and Sherrill, 118-19.
[527] Synan, 119.
[528] Ibid. 130.
[529] Ibid. 53.
[530] FGBMFI, "Let Us Introduce You to the FGBMFI," Full Gospel Business Men's Fellowship International, under "Our Mission Statement," accessed September 25, 2008, http://www.fgbmfi.org, Path: Information.
[531] Demos Shakarian, *A New Wave of Revival: The Vision Intensified* (Costa Mesa: Full Gospel Business Men's Fellowship International, 1992), 5.
[532] Synan, 44.
[533] Ibid. 45.
[534] Shakarian, Sherrill, and Sherrill, 120.
[535] Thomas R. Nickel, *The Shakarian Story* (1964; 3rd ed. comp. Jerry Jensen, repr. Irvine: Full Gospel Business Men's Fellowship International, 1999), 33.
[536] Note: They temporarily named the new group "Full Gospel Business Men's Fellowship of **America**"; Oral Roberts, ed. "Full Gospel Business Men of America Start New National Association," *Healing Waters* (January 1952), 12; Synan, 48; Mathew W. Tallman, *Demos Shakarian: The Life, Legacy, and Vision of a Full Gospel Business Man* (Lexington: Emeth Press, 2010), 143, 153.
[537] Shakarian, Sherrill, and Sherrill, 121.
[538] Around 1992, FGBMFI produced marketing material that implied (and stated) a founding date of 1951, though the context of the word "founded" is more in line with the organization's "beginnings." FGBMFI produced the pamphlet "Let Us Introduce You to the

FGBMFI," which showed a picture of the founder Demos Shakarian and stated that FGBMFI had its "humble **beginnings...in 1951**," and coupled with it, FGBMFI produced another marketing item of a small plastic paper with the title, "Recruiter's Introduction to New Members", which addressed 4 questions including "What is FGBMFI?" The answer: "Members are men of all walks of life, from a great variety of Christian denominations, whose lives are dedicated to God and sharing this knowledge with others. Our members believe the Bible in its entirety, have received Jesus as personal Savior, and believe in the baptism in the Holy Spirit (Acts 2:4). **Founded in 1951**, FGBMFI, a nonprofit organization, has helped literally millions of people find a deeper spiritual life. The Board of Directors consists of volunteer businessmen...." [FGBMFI, "What is FGBMFI?" *Full Gospel Business Men's Fellowship International Recruiter's Introduction to New Members*, n.d. (yet a date of 1992 is derived from its reference to "chapters in 115 countries," which corresponds with the May 1, 1992 publication of the marketing material "Let Us Introduce You to the FGBMFI," and accompanied such brochures)].

539 Shakarian, Sherrill, and Sherrill, 121; Demos Shakarian, 12.
540 Shakarian, Sherrill, and Sherrill, 128-29.
541 Synan, 50.
542 Demos D. Shakarian, "How Our Fellowship Came into Being." *Voice*, February 1953.
543 Shakarian, Sherrill, and Sherrill, 129-30.
544 Ibid. 134.
545 Demos Shakarian, 17.
546 Demos D. Shakarian, "How Our Fellowship Came into Being." *Voice*, February 1953.
547 Synan, 51-52; Shakarian, Sherrill, and Sherrill, 132-35; Tallman, 296.
548 Tallman, 177.
549 Cynthia Shakarian, *The Shakarian Legacy: How a Humble Dairyman Inspired the World!* (Irvine: Shakarian Collective, 2017), 197.
550 Tallman, 147.
551 Nelson B. Melvin, "Who Are We?" *Voice*, January 1984, 39. July 1984, 39.
552 Jerry Jensen, "Who Are We?" *Voice*, November 1985, 39; Jerry Jensen, "Who we Are," *Voice*, February 1995, 18; Jerry Jensen, "Who

Are We?" *Voice*, April 1997, 4. Note: the dating of the founding was removed from *Voice* magazine starting with the mid 1997 editions.

[553] Jerry Jensen, "Who We Are." *Vision: The Dawning of a New Day*, Late 1992, 1.

[554] Nelson B. Melvin, *Voice*, July 1984, 4. Note: the exact date of submitting the documents in California is not known but was obviously after Saturday, November 22, 1952, and probably after Saturday, December 27, 1952, prior to FGBMFI being incorporated on January 2, 1953.

[555] For example, Full Gospel Business Men's *VOICE*, volumes Feb. 1963, Sept. 1967, and July/Aug. 1983.

[556] Richard Shakarian, *Still the Happiest People* (Charlotte: LifeBridge, 2012), Back Cover. Note: Towards the latter years of serving as the FGBMFI's second International President, Richard Shakarian includes a short bio on the back of his book, *Still the Happiest People*, stating that FGBMFI was "founded in 1953 by his late father, Demos Shakarian."

[557] Shakarian, Sherrill, and Sherrill, 137; Synan, 63.

[558] Synan, 68; Tallman, 153.

[559] Shakarian, Sherrill, and Sherrill, 151.

[560] Cynthia Shakarian, 201.

[561] Jerry Jensen, "July 3-8, Miami, Florida," *Voice*, June 1967, 21; Note: Mathematically speaking, since the 10th Annual Convention was held in 1962, then the 14th Annual Convention should have been held in 1966 instead of 1967. Maybe one of the years from 1964 to 1966 did not have a World Convention, or maybe they chose to start counting with the second convention in 1954, with the first "National" Convention in 1953 not being worldwide in scope.

[562] Tallman, 183.

[563] Jerry Jensen, "A Report of the FGBMFI World Convention Youth Revival," *Voice*, September 1971, 35.

[564] Shakarian, Sherrill, and Sherrill, 162.

[565] Mark Bellinger, *Demos: The Man of Fellowship* (Long Beach: Upright Enterprises, 1992), 22.

[566] Bob Armstrong, "Decade of the Seventies," *Celebrate the 50th Year Jubilee Anniversary*, 2003, 24.

[567] Jerry Jensen, "32nd World Convention," *Voice*, June 1985, 34.

ENDNOTES

[568] FGBMFI, "The 1980's—The Decade of Unity," Full Gospel Business Men's Fellowship International, under "Our History," accessed November 23, 2020, http://www.fgbmfi.org.

[569] Tallman, 267; Synan 114. Synan states "by the end of the decade of the 1980's, FGBMFI numbered 2,656 chapters in the world, with 1,800 located in the United States alone."

[570] John Dart, "Worldwide Christian Body Divided Over Funds, Power," *Los Angeles Times*, January 14, 1989.

[571] Tallman, 249; FGBMFI, "Let us Introduce You to the FGBMFI", May 1, 1992.

[572] Tallman, 252.

[573] Richard Shakarian writes that in 2005, the Fellowship was "at work in 156 nations" with 6,000 chapters [Richard Shakarian, *The Art of Multiplication: Explosive Growth!* (Irvine: WWM Inc. 2005), 4.] and in 2012, the Fellowship was in more than 8,000 chapters and 148 countries [Richard Shakarian, *Still the Happiest People*, Back Cover.]

[574] Tallman, 246.

[575] Full Gospel Global Forum, "Welcome to the Full Gospel Global Forum", accessed June 25, 2020, http://www.fg-gf.net/welcome.

[576] Synan, 114.

[577] Tallman, 15.

[578] Executive Ministries, "Home," Executive Ministries, under "Welcome," accessed September 25, 2008, http://www.execmin.org/.

[579] Executive Ministries, "Strategy," Executive Ministries, under "The Dinner Party Outreach," accessed September 25, 2008, http://www.execmin.org/Strategy/dinnerParty.html.

[580] Executive Ministries, "Strategy," under "Speakers with a Clear Message."

[581] Humphreys, *Lasting Investments*, 183.

[582] FCCI, "About," Fellowship of Companies for Christ International, under "About," accessed May 23, 2020, https://fcci.org/about-us/.

[583] Ibid.

[584] FCCI, "Business Leader Groups," Fellowship of Companies for Christ International, under "U.S. – Christ@Work," accessed September 25, 2008, http://www.fcci.org/index.php?option=com_content&task=view&id=34&Itemid=34.

[585] Ministry Watch, "Fellowship of Companies for Christ / FCCI," under "History," accessed May 24, 2020, https://briinstitute.com/mw/ministry.php?ein=581428134.
[586] ICCC, "Home", accessed April 12, 2020, https://iccc.net/.
[587] ICCC, "About ICCC," International Christian Chamber of Commerce, under "Mission Purpose of the ICCC," accessed September 25, 2008, http://www.icccreg.net/pages.asp?pageid=20404.
[588] ICCC, "Home," under "ICCC Vision."
[589] ICCC, "About ICC," accessed April 12, 2020, https://iccc.net/page/ThisisICCC.
[590] ICCC, "Frequently Asked Questions," International Christian Chamber of Commerce, under "16. What is the Difference between ICCC and FGBMFI?" accessed September 25, 2008, http://www.icccreg.net/pages.asp?pageid=20779.
[591] C12 Group, "Buck Jacobs," under "Bio," accessed May 23, 2020, https://www.c12group.com/people/buck-jacobs/.
[592] C12 Group, "About," C12 Group, under "Changing the World" and "More than a CEO Roundtable," accessed April 22, 2020, https://www.c12group.com/about.
[593] Ibid. under "Mission" and "Vision," accessed April 22, 2020, https://www.c12group.com/about.
[594] Ibid. under "The Trusted Authority," accessed April 22, 2020, https://www.c12group.com/about.
[595] C12 Group, "C12 History," C12 Group, under "More than Just a Christian Business Association," accessed September 25, 2008, http://www.c12group.com.
[596] C12 Group, "C12 International Locations," accessed May 23, 2020, https://www.c12group.com/c12-locations/international/.
[597] Miller, *God at Work*, 54.
[598] Pete Hammond, "The Marketplace Movement: Book Titles as a Window," [2004,] under "The 1990s: The Momentum Increases and Diversifies," accessed February 19, 2007, http://www.intheworkplace.com/articles_view.asp?articleid=12875&columnid=1935.
[599] CMDL, "Purpose," Coalition for Ministry in Daily Life, under "Purpose," accessed September 25, 2008, http://www.dailylifeministry.org/Purpose.htm.
[600] Ibid.

ENDNOTES

[601] Hammond, "The Marketplace Movement: Book Titles as a Window," under "The 1990s: The Momentum Increases and Diversifies."

[602] Marketplace Leaders, "About Us," under "Our Vision" and "Our Mission," accessed June 27, 2020, http://www.marketplaceleaders.org/about-us/.

[603] Hillman, *Faith & Work: Do They Mix?* 111.

[604] Marketplace Leaders, "ICWM," under "The International Coalition of Workplace Ministries," accessed April 14, 2020, http://www.marketplaceleaders.org/icwm/.

[605] Ibid.

[606] Hillman, *Faith@Work: What Every Pastor and Church Leader Should Know*, 2.

CHAPTER 13

[607] Ibid. 37.

[608] Hillman, *Faith & Work: Do They Mix?* 37.

[609] Ibid.

[610] Ibid.

[611] Ibid. 38.

[612] Hillman, *Faith@Work: What Every Pastor and Church Leader Should Know*, 53.

[613] Rich Marshall, *God@Work: Discovering the Anointing for Business* (Shippensburg: Destiny, 2000), 5.

[614] Os Hillman, *TGIF: Today God is First*. Shippensburg: Destiny, 2000), 60-84.

[615] Wally Kroeker, preface to *God's Week has 7 Days: Monday Musings for Marketplace Christians*, by Kroeker (Scottdale: Herald, 1998), 14.

[616] Andria Hall, introduction to *The Walk at Work: Seven Steps to Spiritual Success on the Job*, by Hall (Colorado Springs: WaterBrook, 2003), 2.

[617] Barbara Smith-Moran, introduction to *Soul at Work: Reflections on Spirituality of Working*, by Smith-Moran (Winona: Saint Mary's, 1997), 12.

[618] Edward Grube, *Coffee Break Meditations: 260 Devotions for the Workplace* (Saint Louis: CPH, 1997).

[619] Marilyn Kunz and Catherine Schell, *Work—God's Gift: Life Changing Choices* (Dobbs Ferry: Neighborhood Bible Studies, 1993).

[620] Robert Banks and Gordon Preece, *Getting the Job Done Right: 8 Sessions on Developing a Biblical Perspective of Work* (Wheaton: Victor, 1992).

[621] R. Paul Stevens and Gerry Schoberg, *Satisfying Work: Christian Living from Nine to Five*, rev. ed. (Colorado Springs: Shaw-WaterBrook 1993).

[622] Thomas Nelson Publishers, *Making Your Work Count for God: How to Find Meaning and Joy in Your Work*, The Priorities for Living Ser. (Nashville: Thomas Nelson, 1994).

[623] For example, Will Messenger, *Calling and Work* and *Genesis 1-11*.

[624] Wagner, 8.

[625] Ibid.

[626] Os Hillman and Angie Hillman, "Session 5: Unlocking the Kingdom of God in the 9 to 5 Window," *Called to the Workplace—From Esau to Joseph: Living for a Cause Greater Than Ourselves*, 5 CD Audio Series, Marketplace Leaders, 2005.

[627] Hillman, *The 9 to 5 Window*, 64.

[628] Wayne H. House and Thomas Ice, *Dominion Theology: Blessing or Curse?* (Portland: Multnomah, 1988), 419.

[629] Thomas Ice, preface to House and Ice, 9; Albert James Dager, *Vengeance is Ours: The Church in Dominion* (Redmond: Sword, 1990), 179.

[630] Ice, 7.

[631] Ibid. 9.

[632] Dager, 45.

[633] Ibid. 45-46.

[634] Ibid. 180.

[635] Wagner, 39.

[636] Ibid.

[637] *Where We Stand*, 298.

[638] Humphreys, *Lasting Investments*, 36.

[639] Ibid. 24.

[640] Ibid. 43.

[641] Ibid. 44.

[642] Ibid. 53.

[643] Ibid. 54.

[644] R. J. Rushdoony, *Theology of Work: #1 "Vocation & Work" Psalm 126*, Audiocassette, (Chalcedon, 1983).

[645] Ibid.
[646] Bernbaum and Steer, 41-42.
[647] Higginson, under "Is Gift Enough?"
[648] Mills.
[649] 1 Peter 4:10; Matthew 25:14-30; 1 Corinthians 4:2, Luke 12:42-46 and many others.
[650] Bill Hendricks, interview with Theology of Work Project person, *Calling and Giftedness*, podcast audio, 2017, https://soundcloud.com/theology-of-work/giftedness-and-calling-bill.
[651] Will Messenger, *You have Something the World Needs*, audio file, October 18, 2015, https://soundcloud.com/theology-of-work/you-have-something-the-world.
[652] Will Messenger, *What Does it Mean to Hate Your Job?* audio file, 2014, https://soundcloud.com/theology-of-work/what-does-calling-mean-if.
[653] Gordon Preece, "Work," *The Complete Book of Everyday Christianity: An A-To-Z Guide to Following Christ in Every Aspect of Life*, ed. Robert J. Banks and R. Paul Stevens (Downers Grove: InterVarsity, 1997), 1124-25.
[654] Sherman and Hendricks, 86.
[655] Ibid.
[656] Chris Walker, "An Interview with Alistair Mackenzie," *Reality Magazine* 38, 2000, under "The Interviews: A Question of Connectedness," accessed April 12, 2007, http://www.reality.org.nz/articles/38/38-mckenzie.html.
[657] Stevens, 113.

CONCLUSION

[658] Reardon, 50.
[659] Mahaney.
[660] Brian D. McLaren, "3 Mandates to Theology of Work," *The Washington Times*, February 20, 2005, under "Capital Pulpit," accessed April 12, 2007, http://www.washtimes.com/news/2005/feb/20/20050220-100703-6270r/.
[661] Hardy, xvii.
[662] Stuart, 5.
[663] Veith, 63.
[664] Placher, 4.

[665] Dallas Willard, *The Spirit of the Disciplines: Understanding How God Changes Lives*, (San Francisco: Harper, 1988), 214.
[666] Elton Trueblood, *Your Other Vocation* (New York: Harper, 1952), 58.
[667] Rayburn, "Series Introduction: No. 3: The Creation Mandate (Genesis 1:26-28)."
[668] Miller, *God at Work*, 6.
[669] Stevens, 89.
[670] Preece, 1124-25.
[671] Bystrom, 169.
[672] Ibid.
[673] Ibid.

TABLES

[674] Greene, *Thank God it's Monday*, 76.

GLOSSARY

[675] David W. Miller, "The Sunday-Monday Gap: Called to Pew or Profit," January 5, 2005, under "What is a Calling?" accessed February 14, 2007, http://www.yale.edu/faith/esw/x_miller_peworprofit.html.
[676] Helweg, under "Introduction" note 3.
[677] Ibid.
[678] Mahaney.
[679] Humphreys, *Lasting Investments*, 14.
[680] Hillman, *God in the Workplace*.

WORKS CITED

Anglican Church Dioceses of Sydney. "50/95 Theology of Work." 1999. Accessed February 12, 2007. http://www.sydney.anglican.asn.au/synod/synod99/work.html.

Badcock, Gary D. *The Way of Life: A Theology of Christian Vocation.* Eugene: Wipf, 2002.

Banks, Robert J. *God the Worker: Journeys into the Mind, Heart and Imagination of God.* North American ed. 1992. Reprint, Valley Forge: Judson, 1994.

Banks, Robert, and Gordon Preece. *Getting the Job Done Right: 8 Sessions on Developing a Biblical Perspective of Work.* Wheaton: Victor, 1992.

Barnett, Robert. "An Outline of Theological Reflections on the Purpose of Work." December 2003. Accessed December 15, 2006. http://www.gordonconwell.edu/ockenga/mockler/RBarnett_OutlineTheolWork.pdf.

Barth, Karl. *Church Dogmatics: III.4 The Doctrine of Creation.* Edited by G. W. Bromiley and T. F. Torrance. Translated by A. T. Mackay, T. H. L. Parker, H. Knight, H. A. Kennedy, and J. Marks. London: T & T Clark, 2004. Vol. 3. Part 4. Originally published as *Die Kirchliche Dogmatick III: Die Lehre von der Schopfung 4.* (Zurich: Zollikon, 1951).

Beckett, John D. *Loving Monday: Succeeding in Business without Selling Your Soul*. Expanded ed. 1998. Reprint, Downers Grove: IVP, 2006.

Bellinger, Mark, and Hal Donaldson. *Demos: The Man of Fellowship*. Long Beach: Upright Enterprises, 1992.

Bennethum, D. Michael. *Listen! God is Calling! Luther Speaks of Vocation, Faith, and Work*. Minneapolis: Augsburg Fortress, 2003.

Bernbaum, John A. and Simon M. Steer. *Why Work? Careers and Employment in Biblical Perspective*. Grand Rapids: Baker, 1986.

Blumhofer, Edith L. *The Assemblies of God: A Chapter in the Story of American Pentecostalism*. Vol. 2-Since 1941. Springfield: Gospel Publishing House, 1989. 2 vols.

Bosch, David J. *Transforming Mission: Paradigm Shifts in Theology of Mission*. American Society of Missiology Ser. 16. 1991. Reprint, Maryknoll: Orbis, 2005.

Braxton, Lee. "A Dream Comes True." *Voice*, February 1953.

Brook, Linda Rios. *Frontline Christians in a Bottom-Line World*. Shippensburg: Destiny, 2004.

Bryan, Glenn. "The Value of Work: A Case for Promoting Christian Service Opportunities to College Students." May 1991. Accessed January 11, 2007. http://www.cccu.org/resourcecenter/resID.854,parentCatID.89/rc_detail.asp.

Bystrom, Raymond O. "God as Worker: How it Affects Life and Ministry." *Direction* 32, no. 2 (Fall 2003): 166-72. Accessed February 11, 2007. http://www.directionjournal.org/article/?1306.

C12 Group, "About," C12 Group, under "Changing the World" and "More than a CEO Roundtable." Accessed April 22, 2020. https://www.c12group.com/about.

CBMC. "The History of CBMC." CBMC: A Movement of Men. Accessed January 28, 2007. http://www.cbmc.com/about/history.aspx.

Calhoun, Robert, L. "Work and Vocation in Christian History." In *Work and Vocation: A Christian Discussion*. Edited by John Oliver Nelson. 82-115. New York: Harper, 1954.

Chang, Curtis. "Work as Sacrament." June, 4 2004. Accessed February 11, 2007. http://www.the-river.org/resources/Work-as-sacrament.pdf.

Chenu, M. D. *The Theology of Work: An Exploration*. 1963. Translated by Lilian Soiron. Chicago: Regnery, 1966. Originally published as *Pour une Theologie du Travail*. (Paris: Editions du Seuil, [1955]).

CMDL. "Purpose." Coalition for Ministry in Daily Life. Accessed September 25, 2008. http://www.dailylifeministry.org/Purpose.htm.

Colson, Chuck, and Jack Eckerd. *Why America Doesn't Work*. Dallas: Word, 1991.

Cosden, Darrell. *The Heavenly Good of Earthly Work*. United Kingdom: Paternoster P, 2006; Peabody: Hendrickson, 2006.

———. *A Theology of Work: Work and the New Creation*. Eugene: Wipf, 2005.

Criswell, W. A. *Expositor Sermons on Revelation: Five Volumes Complete and Unabridged in One*. Grand Rapids: Zondervan, 1966.

Dager, Albert James. *Vengeance is Ours: The Church in Dominion*. Redmond: Sword, 1990.

Dart, John. "Worldwide Christian Body Divided Over Funds, Power," Los Angeles Times, January 14, 1989.

Davis, John Jefferson. "Will There Be New Work in the New Creation?" *Evangelical Review of Theology* 31, no. 3 (July 2007): 256-73.

Davidson, James. "Why Work? Or 5 Reasons to Get out of Bed on Monday Morning." [July 1996]. Accessed April 9, 2007. http://www.christiansatwork.org.uk/cgi-bin/caw.cgi?&page=resources&rescode=273.

Davidson, James C. and David P. Caddell. "Religion and the Meaning of Work." *Journal for the Scientific Study of Religion* 33, no. 2 (1994): 135-47.

Doorey, Julian. "Faith in the Work Place." *Reality Magazine* 38. 2000. Accessed February 11, 2007. http://www.reality.org.nz/articles/38/38-doorey.html.

Ellul, Jacques. *The Ethics of Freedom*. Translated by Geoffrey W. Bromiley. Grand Rapids: Eerdmans, 1976.

Engstrom, Ted W. and David J. Juroe. *The Work Trap*. Old Tappan: Revell, 1979.

Enlow, David R. *Men Aflame: The Story of CBMC, 1930 – 1965*. 1962; Reprint, Chattanooga: CBMC, 2019.

Executive Ministries. "Home." Executive Ministries. Accessed September 25, 2008. http://www.execmin.org/.

———. "Strategy." Executive Ministries. Accessed September 25, 2008. http://www.execmin.org/Strategy/dinnerParty.html.

FCCI. "About." Fellowship of Companies for Christ International. Accessed May 23, 2020. https://fcci.org/about-us/.

———. "Business Leader Groups." Fellowship of Companies for Christ International. Accessed September 25, 2008. http://www.fcci.org/index.php?option=com_content&task=view&id=34&Itemid=34.

Fee, Gordon D. *The First Epistle to the Corinthians*. Vol. of *The International Commentary on the New Testament*. Grand Rapids: Eerdmans, 1987.

FGBMFI. "Let Us Introduce You To the FGBMFI." Full Gospel Business Men's Fellowship International. Accessed September 25, 2008. http://www.fgbmfi.org. Path: Information.

Friesen, Carly. "Labor: Sin or Sacrament?" *Direction* 10 (1981): 3-13. Accessed January 10, 2007. http://www.directionjournal.org/article/?411.

Gaiser, Frederick J. "What Luther *Didn't* Say about Vocation." *Word & World* 25, no. 4 (Fall 2005): 359-61.

Geldard, M. D. "Work." In *Encyclopedia of Biblical & Christian Ethics*. Rev. ed. Edited by R. K. Harrison. Nashville: Thomas Nelson, 1992.

Gelsinger, Pat. *Balancing Your Family, Faith & Work*. Colorado Springs: Life Journey—Cook Communications, 2003.

Gilbrant, Thoralf, ed. *The Old Testament Hebrew-English Dictionary*. Vol. 7 of *The Complete Biblical Library: The Old Testament Hebrew-English Dictionary*. Edited by Thoralf Gilbrant. Springfield: World Library, 2000.

Goosen, Gideon. *The Theology of Work*. Theology Today Ser. 22. Hales Corners: Clergy Book Service, 1974.

Greene, Mark. "The Great Divide—the Greatest Cultural Challenge Facing the Church." [c. 2000]. Accessed March 29, 2007. http://www.intheworkplace.com/articles_view.asp?articleid=12831&columned =1935.

———. *Thank God it's Monday: Ministry in the Workplace*. 3rd ed. 2001. Reprint, Bletchley, Eng.: Scripture Union, 2003.

Grube, Edward. *Coffee Break Meditations: 260 Devotions for the Workplace*. Saint Louis: CPH, 1997.

Grudem, Wayne. *Systematic Theology: An Introduction to Biblical Doctrine*. Grand Rapids: Zondervan Publishing House, 1994

Guinness, Os. *The Call: Finding and Fulfilling the Central Purpose of Your Life*. Nashville: W Publishing, 2003.

Hall, Andria. Introduction to *The Walk at Work: Seven Steps to Spiritual Success on the Job*. By Hall. Colorado Springs: WaterBrook, 2003. 1-6.

Hammon, Bill. *The Day of the Saints: Equipping Believers for Their Revolutionary Role in Ministry*. 2002. Reprint, Shippensburg: Destiny, 2003.

Hammond, Pete. "Faith at Work is more than Witnessing." November 5, 2004. InterVarsity. Accessed February 21, 2007. http://www.intervarsity.org/news/news.php?item_id=1411.

———. "The Marketplace Movement: Book Titles as a Window." [2004]. Accessed February 19, 2007. http://www.intheworkplace.com/articles_view.asp?articleid=12875&columnid=1935.

Hammond, Pete, R. Paul Stevens, and Todd Svanoe. *The Marketplace Annotated Bibliography: A Christian Guide to Books on Work, Business & Vocation.* Downers Grove: IVP, 2002.

Hardy, Lee. *The Fabric of this World: Inquiries into Calling, Career Choice, and the Design of Human Work.* Grand Rapids: Eerdmans, 1990.

Harper, Keith. Review of *Work in the Spirit: Toward a Theology of Work*, by Miroslav Volf. *Journal of the Evangelical Theological Society* 36 (September 1993): 386-87. Accessed September 28, 2006. http://search.ebscohost.com/login.aspx?direct=true&db=rfh&AN=ATLA0000282041&site=ehost-live.

Harrison, William H. "Loving the Creation, Loving the Creator: Dorothy L. Sayers's Theology of Work." *Anglican Theological Review* 86, no. 2 (Spring 2004): 239-57. Accessed September 28, 2006. http://search.ebscohost.com/login.aspx?direct=true&db=a9h&AN=13117223&site=ehost-live.

Hasel, Gerhard F. *New Testament Theology: Basic Issues in the Current Debate.* Grand Rapids: Wm. B. Eerdmans Publishing Co. 1978.

Haskins, Daniel R. and Yvonne Smith. "Christians in Strategic Leadership: Towards an Integration of Faith and the Top Management Team." October 30, 2004. Accessed March 29, 2007. http://www.cbfa.org/papers/2004conf/Haskins-Smith.doc.

Haywood, Carol L. "Does Our Theology of Work Need Reworking?" *Currents in Theology and Mission* 8 (October 1981): 298-301. Accessed September 28, 2006. http://search.ebscohost.com/login.aspx?direct=true&db=rfh&AN=ATLA0000786949&site=ehost-live.

Helweg, Otto J. "The Secular and Sacred; Friends or Foes?" Accessed February 12, 2007. http://www.leaderu.com/offices/o_helweg/secular_or_sacred.html.

Hendricks, Bill. Interview with Theology of Work Project person. *Calling and Giftedness*. Podcast audio. 2017. https://soundcloud.com/theology-of-work/giftedness-and-calling-bill.

Higginson, Richard. "Worldly Vocation: An Historical Overview." [c. 2000]. Accessed March 29, 2007. http://www.christiansatwork .org.uk/cgi-in/caw.cgi?&page=resources&rescode=268.

Hillman, Os. *The 9 to 5 Window*. Ventura: Regal, 2005.

———. *Are You a Biblical Worker?* Cumming: Aslan, 2003.

———. *Faith@Work: What Every Pastor and Church Leader Should Know*. Cumming: Aslan, 2004.

———. *Faith & Work: Do They Mix?* Alpharetta: Aslan, 2000.

———. *God in the Workplace*. DVD. FaithAndWorkResources.com, 2005.

———. *TGIF: Today God is First*. Shippensburg: Destiny, 2000.

Hillman, Os, and Angie Hillman. *Called to the Workplace—From Esau to Joseph: Living for a Cause Greater Than Ourselves*. Workshop Workbook. [Marketplace Leaders, c. 2005].

———. "Session 5: Unlocking the Kingdom of God in the 9 to 5 Window." *Called to the Workplace—From Esau to Joseph: Living for a Cause Greater Than Ourselves*. 5 CD Audio Series. Marketplace Leaders, 2005.

Hiltner, Seward. "Needed : A New Theology of Work." *Theology Today* 31, no. 3 (October 1974): 243-247. Accessed September 28, 2006. http://search.ebscohost.com/login.aspx?direct=true &db=rfh&AN=ATLA0000748108&site=ehost-live.

Hohne, David. "Work: The Big Picture." *The Briefing* 180. June 1996. Accessed April 10, 2007. http://www.christiansatwork.org.uk/cgi-bin/caw.cgi?&page=resources&rescode=271.

Horton, Stanley M. *The Old Testament Study Bible: Genesis.* Vol. 1 of *The Complete Biblical Library: The Old Testament.* Edited by Thoralf Gilbrant. Springfield: World Library, 1994.

House, H. Wayne, and Thomas Ice. *Dominion Theology: Blessing or Curse?* Portland: Multnomah, 1988.

Hoyt, Herman A. *The End Times.* 1969. Reprint, Winona Lake: BMH, 1995.

Hugenberger, Gordon P. "Is Work the Result of the Fall? A Note on Genesis 2:15." September 2002. Accessed February 11, 2007. http://www.parkstreet.org/pulpit/Work-Genesis2.pdf.

Humphreys, Kent. *Lasting Investments: A Pastor's Guide for Equipping Workplace Leaders to Leave a Spiritual Legacy.* Colorado Springs: NavPress, 2004.

–––. *Shepherding Horses: Understanding God's Plan for Transforming Leaders.* Oklahoma City: Triad Marketing, 2006.

Hunt, Dave. *Whatever Happened to Heaven?* Eugene: Harvest, 1988.

ICCC. "About ICCC." International Christian Chamber of Commerce. Accessed September 25, 2008. http://www.icccreg.net/pages.asp?pageid=20404.

–––. "Frequently Asked Questions." International Christian Chamber of Commerce. Accessed September 25, 2008. http://www.icccreg.net/pages.asp?pageid=20779.

Ice, Thomas. Preface to House and Ice. 7-10.

Imbelli, Robert, P. Review of *Callings: Twenty Centuries of Christian Wisdom on Vocation.* Edited by William C. Placher. *Commonweal* 133, no. 5 (2006): 32-34. Accessed September 28, 2006. http://search.ebscohost.com/login.aspx?direct=true&db=vah&AN=CPLI0000424241&site=ehost-live.

Isaac, Donald J. "Work and Christian Calling." *Direction* 32 (2003): 184-92. Accessed April 11, 2007. http://www.directionjournal.org/article/?1308.

Jensen, David H. *Responsive Labor: A Theology of Work*. Louisville: Westminster, 2006.

Jensen, Jerry. "Who Are We?" *Voice*. November 1985.

John Paul II. *Encyclical Letter On Human Work: Laborem Exercens*. Translated by Vatican. Boston: Pauline, 1981.

Kaiser, Edwin G. *Theology of Work*. Westminster: Newman P, 1966.

Kirk, Gordon. "A Theology of Work: An Encouragement to Employees." Sermon delivered at Lake Avenue Church, Pasadena, CA, July 17, 2004. LAC Sermons Online. Real Audio file. Accessed April 7, 2007. http://www.lakeavefamily.org/audio/wc/2004/20040717wc.rm.

———. "A Theology of Work: Our Work as an Aspect of our Worship." Sermon delivered at Lake Avenue Church, Pasadena, CA, August 1, 2004. LAC Sermons Online. Real Audio file. Accessed April 7, 2007. http://www.lakeavefamily.org/audio/wc/2004/20040801wc.rm.

Kirkland, Wayne. "God's Co-workers." *Reality Magazine* 38. 2000. Accessed April 7, 2007. http://www.reality.org.nz/articles/38/38-kirkland.html.

Kleinhans, Kathryn. "The Work of a Christian: Vocation in Lutheran Perspective." *Word & World* 25, no. 4 (Fall 2005): 394-402.

Kroeker, Wally. Preface to *God's Week has 7 Days: Monday Musings for Marketplace Christians*. By Kroeker. Scottdale: Herald, 1998.

Kunz, Marilyn, and Catherine Schell. *Work—God's Gift: Life Changing Choices*. Dobbs Ferry: Neighborhood Bible Studies, 1993.

Ladd, George Eldon. *A Theology of the New Testament*. Rev. ed. Edited by Donald A. Hagner. Grand Rapids: Wm. B. Eerdmans Publishing Co. 1993.

Larive, Armand. *After Sunday: A Theology of Work*. New York: Continuum, 2004.

Lewis, Jim. "A Theology of Work." The Witness. 2003. Accessed March 9, 2007. http://www.thewitness.org/generalconvention03/TheologyOfWork.ps-.pdf.

Lusk, Rich. "God and Work, Part 2: God Working Through Us, God Working Against Us (Col. 3:22-24; 2 Thess. 3:6-13; Prov. 6:6-11)." Sermon delivered at Trinity Presbyterian Church, Birmingham, AL, June 5, 2005. Trinity Presbyterian Church Sermon Index. MP3 Audio file. Accessed March 29, 2007. http://www.trinity-pres.net/audio/sermon05-06-05.mp3.

Mackenzie, Alistair. "Faith at Work: Vocation, the Theology of Work and the Pastoral Implications." Master's thesis, University of Otago, Dunedin, New Zealand, 1997.

Mackenzie, Alistair, and Wayne Kirkland. *Where's God on Monday? Integrating Faith and Work Every Day of the Week*. Colorado Springs: NavPress, 2003.

Mahaney, C. J. *Why Work?* Quest Tape of the Month. QT161. Audiocassette. [Washington D.C.] 1991.

Marketplace Leaders. "About Us." Marketplace Leaders. Accessed June 27, 2020. http://www.marketplaceleaders.org/about-us/.

Marshall, Paul. "Vocation, Work, and Jobs." *Labour of Love: Essays on Work*, by Paul Marshall, Edward Vanderkloet, Peter Nijkamp, Sander Griffioen, and Harry Antonides. 1-19. Toronto: Wedge, 1980.

Marshall, Rich. *God@Work: Discovering the Anointing for Business*. Shippensburg: Destiny, 2000.

Marshall, Rich, with Ken Walker. *God@Work Volume 2: Developing Ministers in the Marketplace*. Shippensburg: Destiny, 2005.

McDearmid, Andrew. *Eschatology: A Study Guide*. 1980. Reprint, Irving: ICI UP, 1995.

McGregor, Stuart. "Thy Workmate is Thy Neighbor: Essay on the Theology of Work." 2002. Accessed April 11, 2006. http://www.definitive.co.nz/essay/worktheologyresponse.pdf.

McLaren, Brian, D. "3 Mandates to Theology of Work." *The Washington Times*, February 20, 2005. Accessed April 12, 2007. http://www.washtimes.com/news/2005/feb/20/20050220-100703-6270r/.

McLoughlin, Michael. "A New Way to Work: A Paradigm Shift for Marketplace Mission in the 21st Century." [c. 2005]. Accessed February 21, 2007. http://www.intheworkplace.com/articles_view.asp?articleid=12874&columnid=1935.

McLoughlin, Mike, Os Hillman, David W. Miller, and C. Neal Johnson. comp. and eds. *2003 – 2004 International Faith and Work Directory*. Cumming: Aslan, 2003.

Meeks, M. Douglas. *God the Economist: The Doctrine of God and Political Economy*. Minneapolis: Fortress, 1989.

Melvin, Nelson B. "Who Are We?" Voice. January 1984.

Menzies, William W. *Anointed to Serve*. Springfield: Gospel Publishing House, 1971.

Messenger, Will. Executive editor. *Calling and Work*, The Bible and Your Work Study Series. Peabody: Hendrickson Publishers Marketing, 2015.

— — —. Executive editor. *Genesis 1-11*, The Bible and Your Work Study Series. Peabody: Hendrickson Publishers Marketing, 2014.

— — —. Executive editor. *Theology of Work Bible Commentary*, One Volume Edition. Peabody: Hendrickson Publishers Marketing, 2016.

— — —. *What Does it Mean to Hate Your Job?* Audio file. 2014. https://soundcloud.com/theology-of-work/what-does-calling-mean-if.

— — —. You have Something the World Needs. Audio file. October 18, 2015. https://soundcloud.com/theology-of-work/you-have-something-the-world.

Miller, David W. *God at Work: The History and Promise of the Faith at Work Movement*. New York: Oxford UP, 2007.

———. "The Sunday-Monday Gap: Called to Pew and Profit." January 6, 2005. Accessed February 14, 2007. http://www.yale.edu/faith/esw/x_miller_pewandprofit.html.

———. "The Sunday-Monday Gap: Called to Pew or Profit?" January 5, 2005. Accessed February 14, 2007. http://www.yale.edu/faith/esw/x_miller_peworprofit.html.

Mills, Andy. *Part 2: God's Vision for Work*, Audio file. 2014. https://soundcloud.com/theology-of-work/part-2-gods-vision-for-work-1.

Minear, Paul S. "Work and Vocation in Scripture." *Work and Vocation: A Christian Discussion*. Edited by John Oliver Nelson. 32-81. New York: Harper, 1954.

Ministry Watch. "Fellowship of Companies for Christ / FCCI." Accessed May 24, 2020. https://briinstitute.com/mw/ministry.php?ein=581428134.

New American Standard Bible. 1960. Reprint, La Habra, CA: Lockman, 1977.

Nichols, Stephen J. *Martin Luther: A Guided Tour of His Life and Thought*. Phillipsburg: P&R, 2002.

Niebuhr, H. Richard. *Christ and Culture*. New York: HarperCollins, 1951.

Nickel, Thomas R. *The Shakarian Story*, 1964; 3rd ed. Compiled by Jerry Jensen. Reprint, Irvine: Full Gospel Business Men's Fellowship International, 1999.

Oldham, J. H. *Work in Modern Society*. 1950. Reprint, Richmond: John Knox, 1962.

Oppenheimer, Mark. "Miroslav Volf Spans Conflicting Worlds." 2003. Accessed April 11, 2007. http://www.religion-online.org/showarticle.asp?title=2688. Reprint of *The Christian Century* (January 11, 2003): 18-23.

Packer, J. I. *A Quest for Godliness: The Puritan Vision of the Christian Life*. 1990. Reprint, Wheaton: Crossway, 1994.

Pawson, David. "Work." Leadership Development Seminar. August 26, 1993. Audiocassette. Asia Full Gospel Business Men's Fellowship International Convention. Hong Kong Convention Center, Hong Kong.

Peel, William Carr, and Walt Larimore. *Going Public with Your Faith: Becoming a Spiritual Influence at Work*. Grand Rapids: Zondervan, 2003.

Pentecost, J. Dwight. *Things to Come: A Study in Biblical Eschatology*. 1958. Reprint, Grand Rapids: Zondervan.1977.

Pieper, Josef. *Leisure, the Basis of Culture*. Translated by Gerald Malsbary. 1948. Reprint, South Bend: St. Augustine's, 1998.

Placher, William C. Introduction to *Callings: Twenty Centuries of Christian Wisdom on Vocation*. Edited by William C. Placher. Grand Rapids: Eerdmans, 2005.

Preece, Gordon. "Work." In *The Complete Book of Everyday Christianity: An A-To-Z Guide to Following Christ in Every Aspect of Life*. Edited by Robert J. Banks and R. Paul Stevens. Downers Grove: InterVarsity, 1997.

Rayburn, Robert S. "Retirement (Eccles. 12:1-5)." Theology of Work Ser. Rec. June 4, 2006. Faith Presbyterian Church, Tacoma, WA.

— — —. "Series Introduction: No. 3: The Creation Mandate (Genesis 1:26-28)." Theology of Work Ser. Rec. 9 Apr. 2006. Faith Presbyterian Church, Tacoma, WA.

Reardon, Patrick T. "Good Job!" *U.S. Catholic* 68, no. 9 (September 2003): 50.

Richardson, Alan. *The Biblical Doctrine of Work*. Ecumenical Biblical Studies No. 1. 1952. Reprint, London: SCM, 1954.

Ringma, Charles. "Tensions in a Theology of Work." July 1998. Accessed October 20, 2007. http://www.christiansatwork.org.uk/cgi-bin/caw.cgi?&page=resources&rescode=233.

Robinson, Haddon W. Foreword to *Theology of Work Bible Commentary*, One Volume edition, executive edited by Will Messenger, xxv-xxviii. Peabody: Hendrickson Publishers Marketing, 2016.

Roseman, James M. "Toward a Theology of Work and Business: Reflections on Christianity, Calling, and Commerce." October 3, 2003. Accessed October 20, 2007. http://www.dbu.edu/naugle/pdf/Towards1.pdf.

Rossier, Bernard. "Verse-by-Verse Commentary on Ephesians, Philippians, Colossians, Philemon." *The New Testament Study Bible: Galatians-Philemon*. Vol. 8 of *The Complete Biblical Library*. Edited by Thoralf Gilbrant. Springfield: Complete Biblical Library, 1989.

Rushdoony, R. J. *Theology of Work: #1 "Vocation & Work" Psalm 126*. Audiocassette. Chalcedon, 1983.

Ryken, Leland. *Redeeming the Time: A Christian Approach to Work & Leisure*. Grand Rapids: Baker, 1995.

Sailhamer, John H. "Genesis." In vol. 7 of *The Expositor's Bible Commentary*. Edited by Frank E. Gaebelein. 1-284. Grand Rapids: Zondervan, 1990.

Sayers, Dorothy L. *Are Women Human?* 1971. Reprint, Grand Rapids: Eerdmans, 2005.

———. *The Mind of the Maker*. 1941. Reprint, New York: HarperCollins, 1979.

———. "Why Work?" In *Creed or Chaos?* 1949. Reprint, Manchester: Sophia, 1974. 63-84.

Schultz, Samuel J. "Verse-by-Verse Commentary on Obadiah, Micha, Haggai, Zechariah, Malachi." *The Old Testament Study Bible: Daniel-Malachi*. Vol. 15 of *The Complete Biblical Library: The Old Testament*. Edited by Thoralf Gilbrant. Springfield: Complete Biblical Library, 1999.

Schuurman, Douglas J. *Vocation: Discerning Our Callings in Life*. Grand Rapids: Eerdmans, 2004.

Shakarian, Cynthia. *The Shakarian Legacy: How a Humble Dairyman Inspired the World!* Irvine: Shakarian Collective, 2017.

Shakarian, Demos. *A New Wave of Revival: The Vision Intensified.* Costa Mesa: Full Gospel Business Men's Fellowship International, 1992.

Shakarian, Demos, with John Sherrill and Elizabeth Sherrill. *The Happiest People on Earth.* Chappaqua: Steward Press, 1975.

Shakarian, Demos D. "How Our Fellowship Came into Being." *Voice.* February 1953.

Shakarian, Richard. *Still the Happiest People.* Charlotte: LifeBridge, 2012.

Sherman, Doug, and William Hendricks. *Your Work Matters to God.* 1987. Reprint, Colorado Springs: NavPress, 1988.

Silvoso, Ed. *Anointed for Business.* Ventura: Regal, 2002.

Simmons, Laura K. *Creed without Chaos: Exploring Theology in the Writings of Dorothy L. Sayers.* Grand Rapids: Baker, 2005.

Smith, Lee J. "A Biblical Theology of Work." [c. 2002]. Accessed February 11, 2007. http://www.randolphefree.org/monographtheowork.htm.

Smith, Nancy R. *Workplace Spirituality: A Complete Guide for Business Leaders.* Peabody: Axial Age, 2006.

Smith-Moran, Barbara. Introduction to *Soul at Work: Reflections on Spirituality of Working.* By Smith-Moran. Winona: Saint Mary's, 1997.

Stanley, Andy. "Part 1: Meet the Boss." *Taking Care of Business: Finding God at Work.* DVD. North Point Ministries, Inc. 2005.

Stevens, R. Paul. *The Other Six Days: Vocation, Work, and Ministry in Biblical Perspective.* Grand Rapids: Eerdmans, 2000; Vancouver, BC: Regent College, 2000. Reprint. of *The Abolition of the Laity.* 1999.

Stevens, R. Paul, and Gerry Schoberg. *Satisfying Work: Christian Living from Nine to Five*. Rev. ed. Colorado Springs: Shaw-WaterBrook, 1993.

Still, Todd D. "Did Paul Loathe Manual Labor? Revisiting the Work of Ronald F. Hock on the Apostle's Tentmaking and Social Class." *Journal of Biblical Literature* 125, no. 4 (Winter 2006): 781-95.

Stuart, Peter. "Christians in the Workplace: A Practical Theology of Work." Latimer Occasional Paper No. 6. Christchurch, New Zealand: Latimer Fellowship. November 2000. Accessed April 7, 2007. http://www.latimer.org.nz/downloads/theology-work.pdf.

Synan, Vinson. *Under His Banner: History of Full Gospel Business Men's Fellowship International*. Costa Mesa: Gift, 1992.

Tallman, Mathew W. *Demos Shakarian: The Life, Legacy, and Vision of a Full Gospel Business Man*. Lexington: Emeth Press, 2010.

Tamasy, Robert J. Introduction to *Jesus Works Here*. Edited by Tamasy. Nashville: Broadman, 1995.

———. *Marketplace Ambassadors: CBMC's Continuing Legacy of Evangelism and Disciplemaking*. Chattanooga: Christian Business Men's Connection, 2019.

Tenney, Merrill C. *New Testament Survey*. Rev. ed. by Walter M. Dunnett. 1985. Reprint, Grand Rapids: Eerdmans, 1996; Leicester, England: IVP, 1996.

Theology of Work Project. "Theology of Work Project." Theology of Work Project. Accessed October 2, 2008 and November 27, 2020. http://www.theologyofwork.org.

Thomas Nelson Publishers. *Making Your Work Count for God: How to Find Meaning and Joy in Your Work*. The Priorities for Living Ser. Nashville: Thomas Nelson, 1994.

Thompsett, Fredrica Harris. Review of *After Sunday: A Theology of Work*, by Armand Larive. *Anglican Theological Review* 87, no. 4 (2004): 703-06. Accessed September 28, 2006. http://www.epnet.com.

Tozer, A.W. *The Pursuit of God*. Harrisburg: Christian, 1948.

Trueblood, Elton. *Your Other Vocation*. New York: Harper, 1952.

Veith, Gene Edward, Jr. *God at Work: Your Christian Vocation in All of Life*. Wheaton: Crossway, 2002.

Volf, Miroslav. "God at Work." *Word & World* 25, no. 4 (Fall 2005): 381-93.

— — —. *Work in the Spirit: Toward a Theology of Work*. 1991. Reprint, Eugene: Wipf, 2001.

Wagner, Peter C. *The Church in the Workplace*. Ventura: Regal, 2006.

Wallis, Arthur. Foreword to *Serving Christ in the Workplace: Secular Work is Full-Time Service*. By Larry Peabody. Fort Washington: CLC, 2004. Reprint of *Secular Work is Full-time Service*. 1974.

Walker, Chris. "An Interview with Alistair Mackenzie." *Reality Magazine* 38. 2000. Accessed April 12, 2007. http://www.reality.org.nz/articles/38/38-mckenzie.html.

Walvoord, John F. *The Revelation of Jesus Christ*. 1966. Reprint, Chicago: Moody, 1978.

Warren, Rick. *The Purpose Driven Life: What on Earth am I Here For?* Grand Rapids: Zondervan, 2002.

Where We Stand: The Official Position Papers of the Assemblies of God. Springfield: Gospel, 2003.

Willard, Dallas. *The Spirit of the Disciplines: Understanding How God Changes Lives*. San Francisco: Harper, 1988.

Wingren, Gustaf. *Luther on Vocation*. Translated by Carl C. Rasmussen. Eugene: Wipf, 1957.

Zabocki, Ed. "A Theology of Work for Changing Times." [c. 2000]. Accessed April 11, 2007. http://www.nafra-sfo.org/work_commission_resources/wrkart10.html.

Zalot, Jozef D. Review of *After Sunday: A Theology of Work*, by Armand Larive. *Theological Studies* 66, no. 3 (2005): 718-19. Accessed September 28, 2006. http://search.ebscohost.com/login.aspx?direct=true&db=aph&AN=18032281&site=ehost-live.

Zeigler, J. R. "Full Gospel Business Men's Fellowship International." *The New International Dictionary of Pentecostal and Charismatic Movements*. Edited by Stanley M. Burgess. Rev. and Exp. ed. Grand Rapids: Zondervan, 2002.

ABOUT THE AUTHOR

DOUGLAS E. WOOLLEY works for JPMorgan Chase & Co. as a Software Engineer, and he serves as the International Secretary for the Full Gospel Business Men's Fellowship International (FGBMFI). He earned four university degrees in the areas of Computer Science and Theology.

DOUGLAS E. WOOLLEY graduated from University of South Florida in 1989 with a B.S. Engineering degree in Computer Science. Upon graduation, Doug worked as a part of the Management Association Program at NCNB (now known as Bank of America). Doug worked for Verizon (formerly GTE) for 28 years, most recently as a Web Developer in the field of Cloud Computing and has attained three prestigious certifications in Amazon Web Services (AWS). While at Verizon, he also traveled often to Portugal and to Venezuela to install and implement a new computer software system that produced phone bills for these countries. As of 2019, he currently works for JPMorgan Chase & Co. as a Software Engineer. He recently finished a B.S. degree in Computer Information Systems with a concentration in Web Development (from DeVry University), *Summa Cum Laude*.

In high school, Doug placed among the top in the USA in mathematics, computer programming, and science. As a senior in high school, Doug placed 1st in Florida in both mathematics and computer science, was team captain of the top computer-programming team in Florida, and placed 3rd in (individual) mathematics and 5th in (team) computer-programming at the national championships for Mu Alpha Theta. The Westinghouse Talent Search named him as one of the top

300 high school scientists in America for his computer program that graphically solves the Rubik's Cube and other mathematical puzzles. By the age of 20, Doug began receiving royalties for providing computer-programming illustrations for two university textbooks on computers, and later he authored an 800-page computer-programming book. Additionally, he is a member of American Mensa.

As a committed Christian, Doug has a passion for studying and teaching the Bible. He has led weekly Bible studies for years with interested college students, church members, co-workers, and ministry interns. He also graduated with a B.S. in Interdisciplinary Studies (concentration in Bible/Theology) at North Central University, *Summa Cum Laude*. He earned a master's degree in Bible/Theology at Southwestern A/G University, *with a 4.0 GPA*. Serving in his local church, Life Church, Doug has taught Sunday School for the New Believers class and the Singles class. Further, Doug has taught college level Bible courses at two different Schools of Ministry.

Doug has served in various leadership positions in Full Gospel Business Men's Fellowship International (FGBMFI) since 1991, such as vice-president of the Tampa chapter, Florida Treasurer and Field Representative, International Director at Large, USA National Director, and Web Master for www.fgbmfi.org and regional sites. He has performed missionary work in multiple countries and has been a key speaker at national conventions. Currently, Doug serves as USA Southeast Regional Director, International Director, and International Secretary (one of four executive positions for FGBMFI).

Doug resides in Tampa, Florida, USA with his wife Marsha and poodle Napoleon. Some of Doug's hobbies include running with his dog, golfing, competing in international programming competitions, and fine dining. Marsha Woolley served as Director of Women's Ministries for the A/G in the Peninsular Florida District, serving 350 churches. Currently, she serves as a manager of a retail department store. More information can be seen on Doug's personal website: www.DouglasWoolley.com

CPSIA information can be obtained
at www.ICGtesting.com
Printed in the USA
LVHW051815220321
682109LV00022B/1148